Fun With Lord Oaksey

Incorporating
'Funny & Memorable Times in Horseracing'

Alwin 'Bobby' Watts

To LYNDSEY

ALL THE BEST

Alwin

A Bright Pen Book

British Library Cataloguing Publication Data.
A catalogue record for this book is available from the British Library

ISBN 978- 0-7552-1542-3

Authors OnLine Ltd
19 The Cinques
Gamlingay, Sandy
Bedfordshire SG19 3NU
England

This book is also available in eBook format, details of which are available at www.authorsonline.co.uk

Acknowledgements

Lady Oaksey for her permission to write the book and for her help.

Jack Berry for doing the forward, and I admire his work for the injured jockeys.

Many thanks to Nora Watts for her help with the preparation of this book.

The author aged about 19

Forward

It has been a pleasure and a delight to write the forward to Alwin's amazing book. In racing, especially working in the yards, I can assure you there is much more fun going on than simply mucking out or riding exercise in the cold, miserable wet weather.

As shown by the true stories in Alwin's book, some of the recollections will make your sides ache with laughter when you read the stunts and pranks racing personnel try on each other.

Alwin is not unlike many of the horses, he is keen to please.
I sincerely hope when you read 'Fun with Lord Oaksey' you will be enthralled.

Proceeds from the book will be donated to the Injured Jockeys Fund, which the late and great Lord Oaksey, a founder trustee of the IJF would have been delighted with.

Now sit back and enjoy the book.

Jack Berry MBE
Vice President IJF

Contents

John 'Lord Oaksey's' Wedding

When "Lord Oaksey" got married to Major Ginger Dennistoun's daughter Victoria, known as "Tory", we were all invited to the wedding, and even had a invitation card. Major Dennistoun arranged for a coach to take us all to the Temple Bar off Fleet Street in London, where the wedding took place. When we arrived at the church a man called Jimmy Blunt was waiting for us and approached Tony Perkins and myself. He asked us to go and have a drink in Fleet Street at the tavern he knew. We walked through an archway into Fleet Street, turned left, and drinks were waiting for us on the bar. Whilst having a drink with Jimmy, we more or less forgot about the wedding until suddenly the church bells began to ring. We downed our drinks and rushed back to the church. When we got there Tony looked for his wife. She was already in the church and when we spotted her she was looking around with an angry expression on her face. She had kept two seats for us and before Tony even sat down she started to tell him off. The people in the pew behind told her to keep quiet but she kept on and on.

"Tony, how could you leave me on my own like that? Where have you been?" Tony just sat there with the big grin on his face throughout the ticking off.

After the service we all went over to the church hall which was right next door. As we went into the hall we were handed glasses of champagne. However whilst we were drinking the champagne, Tony said, "We must get something better to drink!" So we went over and chatted to one of the waiters. We gave him the name of a horse to back and he came back with a bottle of malt whisky and two glasses. We sat quietly drinking the malt whisky in a corner. Then Major Dennistoun came up to us.

"Tony, where did you get the malt whisky from?" he asked.

Tony replied, "I got it from the waiter."

"It's my malt whisky," said the Major, "and I can't have any of it!"

Tony replied, "You can have some Major," But he didn't!

After the wedding, I remember everybody came out of the hall to wave goodbye and take photographs and John "Lord Oaksey" was stood up in a brand new Ford Consul convertible.

After that we all got back on the coach, ready to return to Letcombe Regis. However by the time we were on the way back I began to feel really ill. Luckily I was sitting by the open window because during the journey I was eventually sick. Unfortunately Mrs. Simons was sat behind me and the sick was blown back across the bus onto her face. She wasn't very happy.

When we got back to Letcombe Regis, Tony Perkins invited Jim Simons and myself for a drink - I had tea!

Tony said, 'I don't feel very good. I've got a bad head!'

Barbara replied, 'Serves you right!'

'I'm going to bed,' said Tony

Jim said to Tony, "I know what you need to put you right - a couple of a raw eggs in some milk. Swallow it straight down."

I looked at Jim, watching what he was doing.

He pick up a fresh egg out of a tray and as he got the egg in his hands, which were not very steady and nor were his feet, he missed the glass and broke the egg over the table.

Tony said, "There's another egg." After six eggs he ended up with one egg in the glass and lots of broken eggs on the floor.

It was time for me to say thank you to Tony and I was off to my lodgings.

Guests at John Lawrence's first wedding 1957
(the author far left)

A Knowing Head Lad

The head lad waited on the hack at the bottom of the gallop and told each lad in turn what he had to do with his horse as he rode by.

'John, Jim, Peter and Paul, you go a nice steady canter up five furlongs, one behind the other, and Paul, if you can't hold your horse, pull him up.' Paul answered the head lad, 'but if I can't hold my horse, I won't be able to pull him up.'

'Ha! Paul I can see you're the brainy one here. You'll be telling me next what's going to win the overnight seller at Bogside. You, Paul, are going to go a long way in a long time. Now get on with it and not so much chat.'

The trainer remarked, 'The horse looks very well and moves like a flying machine.'

'Yes, he moves alright,' answered the wise old lad, 'but he's always going to carry two stone too many,'

'Why do you say that?' asked the trainer.

'Because until he puts his mind to the right things he will not be a lot of good.'

'Well what would you do about him?' asked the trainer.

'There is only one thing you can do; introduce him to a sharp knife, then all his troubles will be over!' replied the wise old lad laughing.

A Ladder a Bit Too Long

This is a true story about an apprentice called Vic.

At the end of the racing season the stable yard and the horse boxes are cleaned and sometimes repainted.

Vic was asked to go and get the ladder from the tack room. After about half an hour, Vic still had not turned up with the ladder so I went to find out what had happened to him and why he had been so long. When I got to the tack room he had got the ladder stuck across the doorway. I asked him what was the matter and almost in tears he said that the ladder was too big to go through the door. I had to put him right!

At the evening stable time when the Major did his inspection round, Vic was asked if he had had any trouble with a ladder and straight away Vic replied that if I had not helped him out he would still be there. With a smile on his face the Major said, 'So, it was true then.'

The Little Things

When all the lads and the apprentices come to the feed room to get the food for the horses, they have to wait in a line for their turn to get it from the head lad. This would be an opportunity to check with each lad as to the condition of the horses in his care. When it got to a lad called Darky the head lad looked at him and said, 'Your horse is a very clever horse.'

'Yes,' said Darky, 'how do you know that?'

'Because you leave the light on every night so that he can read *The Sporting Life*. Now turn that light out like every one else. We don't want him going f...... cross-eyed do we?'

Pigeon's Milk

One of Frank's favourite tricks was to send a new apprentice to go and get a pint of pigeon's milk at the village shop. When the apprentice asked the lady in the shop for the milk she would just give him ten cigarettes. The apprentice would say, 'But I wanted a pint of pigeon's milk'

'Yes,' she always replied, 'but there's no pigeon's milk today'. With a smile she would add, 'Don't forget to tell Frank that he owes me for those cigarettes'.

When the apprentice returned to the stable yard he gave the cigarettes to Frank. 'Where's the pigeon's milk then?' he would ask.

The apprentice told him the pigeons had not laid any for the past three days.

'That's a bloody nuisance,' said Frank, 'How's my horse supposed to win now!'

The Two Shilling Race

With any group of people there's always a lot of banter and fun talking, no less so in stables and racing.

All the stable lads have nicknames. Here are a few: 'Roger the Dodger'. He was always getting out of cleaning and sweeping the yard or cutting the chaff. 'Darky', because of his dark hair; 'Bomber', his trade mark was to wear an RAF helmet whereas we mainly wore flat caps before the riding helmet was introduced. 'Flash the Lad', because he wore bright ties. Myself, I was called the 'Professor' or 'Ol'.

Mr Robin Lord would always call me Professor. He was my racing valet. He would always greet me by saying, 'Good morning, Professor, what can we do for you today?' I never did find out why he called me that but we always got on very well and he helped me out a lot.

As I say there is always a lot of banter and one day at the end of the morning's work we were all cleaning our tack with silver sand which was kept in a large bucket at the end of the tack room. Of course, when we were all in there together cleaning our tack the older lads would be saying things like, 'That new apprentice is a better runner than Roger the Dodger.' The older lads would start off by saying that Flash was a better runner than Roger the Dodger and then Darky would say, 'He can't beat me.' This kind of talk went on and on until the head lad said, 'Right, we'll settle this, we'll have a race down in the bottom paddock.' Then he put his hand into his pocket and pulled out a two shilling piece, and held it up so we could all see it. He walked over to the silver sand bucket and dropped the two shillings into it. (The silver sand was used to clean the metal bits on the bridle.)

'Right', he said, 'we'll have a 50 yard run at the end of this evening stable time - the first to get to the bucket gets the two shillings.' That was a lot of money in those days, as I earned only five shillings a week. Well of course I said I would run too.

When we were all lined up at the start there were about eleven of us altogether. One of the older lads had taken a liking to me. He was called 'Chips' because he had a face like Scaramouch. Chips was asked to be at the start and line us all up. The head lad brought out the silver sand bucket and put it down about 50 yards from the start. When we lined up Chips told me to stand by him on the outside. He said that I would be bumped by the others and he would make sure that I got a good start. Chips put his hand up and shouted, 'Are you ready? Get set! Go!' Off I went to run like hell and at the same time Chips put his foot out and tripped me up. As I picked myself up I shouted at Chips, 'What did you do that for?'

Chips just smiled and said, 'Just you wait and see.'

We both watched the finish of the race. Four apprentices got there together and all dived for the bucket. The bucket shot up into the air - the silver sand had been changed for horse dung and water and it came down all over them. They looked a sorry sight. To be fair to the head lad, he gave all the apprentices a two shilling piece each. After that I was very careful not to be caught out by that type of joke.

Caught in the Act

When I first started as an apprentice one of my jobs was to go round with the Major, the trainer and the head lad with a bucketful of carrots so the Major could give one to each horse when he had a look at them. We would go from one horse box to another. The Major would feel the horse's legs and check along its back and would also take note of how it had been groomed. Each lad would take up all the straw bedding and make up a square pile in the corner of the box and on top of this the lad would place his grooming kit. A twist in the straw was placed across the doorway. Just in front of the twisted straw the lad would knock out the dust from the curry comb and make a nice row of piles of dust. The more dust piles there were the better because that was an indication of the hard work gone into grooming the horse. As soon as the Major had gone the lad would clean up the dust and put it into a matchbox or a little tin to put it out the next night.

I will always remember there was a lad who kept his horse box top door shut at evening stable time. When the Major came to his box he would not bother to see the horse because it always sounded like it was in a bad temper, upset or did not liked being groomed.

We could all hear sounds coming from the horse box: 'Whoa! Stand still, that's enough!' as well as the loud banging. When the lad came to get the feed for the horse the head lad would ask him if he felt all right on his own with such a bad tempered horse. 'It's OK,' the lad would reply, 'it's a good job that I can keep him in check.'

One night when the Major was doing his rounds I followed as usual. We could hear the noise coming from the horse box again and the Major said, 'I must see this horse tonight.' He very slowly opened the top door of the horse box and there was the old horse tied to the wall looking half asleep. We could still hear the 'Whoa there!' and the banging and the shouting. 'Stand still!'

The Major shouted out, 'What the hell are you doing, Ted?' And there was Ted sitting on a pile of straw with a curry comb in his hand knocking it against the wall shouting, 'Stand still!'

'I was only having a joke,' said Ted, as quick as a flash.

The One They Could not Catch

One of the best jokes I have seen was about a twiggie stick. Jack Prendergast was one of the head lads in charge of the yearlings' yard. This particular year we had a yearling arrive that was very nervous about having his head touched so we had a job to get a head collar on him. When the Major saw that he had no collar on he asked Jack why. Jack told him that the horse was very nervous about having his head touched and that he wanted to let the horse settle down first before he made the attempt. This went on for a few days and in the end the Major said, 'This is not good enough, Jack, we have to get a head collar on him some how. He must have had one on him when he came'.

The very next evening he had a brand new head collar on and I had even plaited his fore top and mane. He looked very smart. The Major asked Jack how he had managed to put the head collar on him. Jack said, 'I went and got a twiggie stick out of the hedge and held the head collar on the end of it and then lowered it over his head and it was on.'

'Well done, Jack,' said the Major. Jack stuck his chest out and took all the credit for the head collar being on the yearling. Of course he did not know how it was done.

Well, it's easy when you know how to do these things with yearlings or foals. It took us just two seconds to do it. First off the yearling had a head collar on his head as soon as he arrived but we found that there was something wrong with it so we took it off again. When the evening stable time came he still didn't have the head collar back on. Jack tried to put it on just before the Major came to look round but couldn't so he left it off.

When we took the yearling out and brought him back in we left the head collar off for a laugh.

On the day of the Christmas party Jim Foff, one of the lads that worked on breaking the yearling, asked the Major if when he made his speech at the dinner party he would please give Jack Prendergast this present on behalf of all the lads in the yard, and would he ask Jack to open it there and then. The present was a box just over two foot long and two inches by four inches.

The Major finished his speech by saying how well we had done that year and how we would have an even better one next year and gave us all a vote of thanks. He then said, 'There is just one thing more I must do. I give this present to Jack Prendergast from all the lads.'

Jack stood up and walked right down the centre of the hall and up to the Major to receive the present. He thanked the Major and went back to his seat. The Major said, 'Well Jack, open it so that we can all see what you have got.' Jack undid the box and held out a twiggie stick. His face went red and we all fell about laughing. Jack took it really well and even laughed himself!

The Pigs

The Major came up to the yard and called me. He said, 'Quick, get some bales of straw and bring them down to the paddock.'

I got the wheelbarrow and loaded it up with bales of straw and took it down. The Major then said, 'That's not enough, get some more'.

When I brought the next load the Major was pulling a large sheet of corrugated tin from the back of his Landrover. 'Come on, give me a hand,' he shouted at me.

I asked him what he was doing. 'Making a piggery of course, you silly ass.' (Silly ass was one of his favourite sayings.) We made a pen with the corrugated tin on the top of the bales of straw. Just as we finished the pig pen the small piglets arrived. The little pigs began to grow and always looked well. They became quite tame so we could pick them up and carry them around in our arms. The Major didn't know this, or how tame the pigs had become. One cold evening when there was a moon so bright you could see quite well outside, Tony and I were sitting in his bungalow which was not too far from the Major's house. We were both a bit bored so we went out to look at the little pigs. Somehow we got the idea of taking two of the pigs and putting them into the Major's house. By now there was a sharp frost.

We waited until all the lights in the Major's house had gone out. While we were waiting we made a plan.

First we decided to get the key, lock the main door and leave the key in the door on the outside. We wanted to make a lot of noise, so we found a couple of bricks and some string and we tied the bricks to the horn of the Landrover. We had to make sure that no one could get out of the kitchen door. This door didn't have a key but just outside the kitchen there were three snow sledges so we tied them to the door handle. The main door had a doorbell on the side, so it was easy to put a stick across the doorway and keep the pressure on the bell button so that it would keep ringing.

There was a big moon shining. About half an hour after the lights went out in the Major's house we tied the snow sledges to the handle on the kitchen door, then put the bricks and the string by the Landrover, placed the stick by the main door and took the door key from the inside of the door and locked it on the outside to make sure it worked OK. We left the key on the outside ready to lock. We went and got a pig each and carried it in our arms back to the Major's house. We crept into the house and up the stairs and put both pigs into the Major's bedroom. Then we ran out of the house as quickly as we could. Tony put the bricks onto the Landrover's horn and tied them on tight with the string - at the same time I put the stick across the front doorway and tight onto the bell button. The noise was good and loud and it frightened the pigs. We could hear them squeaking.

The Major started to shout. 'Nancy, Ginny, stop that bloody bell and get these pigs out of our bedroom!' The lights went on all over the house and we saw Ginny run past the upstairs windows and down to the main door. She called out, 'Daddy, I can't open the door, it's locked.'

'Well find the key or go out the kitchen door,' shouted back the Major. Ginny could only open the kitchen door a little way but she could not get out. She then ran back towards the stairs shouting, 'Daddy, Daddy! I can't get out of the kitchen door.'

Well get out of a window then!' shouted back the Major.'

Ginny, the Major's daughter, was about 17 years old at that time. The next thing we saw was a bare bum coming out of the window for Ginny was only wearing a very small, frilly, silk night dress. I stood open mouthed; Tony gave me a tug on my arm and whispered, "it's time we went'.

The next morning the Major came marching up to Tony and me to ask if we had heard anything in the night. We said, 'No, why?'

'Because some silly ass was playing a joke last night,' he shouted at us. 'Someone put two pigs into the house and the stink and mess is terrible. The pigs squirted shit straight up the curtains in the bedroom and all down the stairs. Who do you think did it?'

I said, 'It sounds like it could have been Michael or John Lawrence; they are the only ones I can think of Major.'

His face went red and he shouted back at me. 'Of course it wasn't Michael, he's in Ireland.'

A few weeks later, when we were in the car going to the races, just to get the Major going, I asked if he had found out who had put the pigs into his house. He replied angrily, 'If I find out who did it, I'll make them wish they had never been born.' His voice got louder and louder as he bit down on his pipe. 'The smell is still in the house and the stain on the carpet is still there,' he shouted.

I nearly burst out laughing. How I didn't I will never know. I must say that the most memorable thing about it all which I will always see in my mind is Ginny coming out of the window in just a frilly pink night dress. It was the first time I had seen a lady's bare bum.

Lose Weight the Hard Way

The Major had a horse running at Newton Abbot in August, one of the first jump meetings of the season. I travelled with the horse and we started a horsebox with some of F.W's horses from Lambourn. It took nearly all day to get to Newton Abbot at that time.

On the way one of the lads from the F.W. yard, named Aly Blanford, asked the driver Micky Fin if he knew of a good way to lose weight.

'Why?' asked Micky, looking across at him and not straight ahead at the road in front.

'Because I've got a ride tomorrow and I have to do ten stone. I am much too heavy.'

'Well, how much have you to lose?' asked Micky.

'About 8 to 10lbs.'

'The only thing I can suggest is for you to buy some Ex-lax from a chemist.'

'Will you stop at a chemist if you see one?' asked Aly.

As soon as we came to the next town Micky stopped the horsebox and put his head out of the window and shouted out to a man on the other side of the road. 'Hey, do you know where the chemist is?'

The man looked a bit vague and said, 'No.'

Micky shouted back at him, 'You know nothing and you have the gall to have lived as long as you have!' Off we went along the road a little further until we could see a chemist right in front of us. Before the horsebox had come to full stop, Aly was out of it and running towards the shop. A few minutes later out he came, stuffing the chocolate Ex-lax into his mouth. Off we went again, Aly still eating the chocolate. Micky turned and asked him how much he had eaten. 'Only two large bars,' said Aly.

'Well, you're sure going to know the good Lord gave you an asshole, Aly.'

As soon as the horsebox stopped off went Aly looking for a toilet. After we had all seen to the horses we went across the road to a row of terraced cottages where we were to lodge. I must say the hospitality was excellent, wonderful food and very comfortable. As soon as we were in the cottage the lady of the house asked us if we would like a nice cup of tea. We sat down and soon poor Aly started to get pains in his stomach. He said he was very thirsty and could drink a whole pot of tea. We told him not to eat or drink as it would make him ill and put weight on. He had two cups of tea then ran to the toilet and was still there when we were going to go out up to the town for the evening. I knocked on the toilet door to see if he would like to come with us. In a sad voice he said, 'I can't leave this toilet, every time I go to come out I have to go again.'

When we came back he was still in the toilet and he sounded very tired. The next day Aly looked like death warmed up; he did not eat anything until after the race. I must say I thought he did very well to finish the race at all. He came in third place and only put up one pound over weight.

Wet Romance

I went to the Devon and Exeter meeting and we shared the horsebox with F.W. Their travelling head lad was Darky Letham. He asked me if I had arranged anywhere to stay overnight. I said I would ask the man in charge of the stable yard if he could recommend somewhere.

'Well,' said Darky, 'one of the horses we were going to run is not now, and I had booked for four lads to stay with Mrs H. in her lovely house. If you like you can stay there and make up the number.' I accepted the offer and Darky went on to tell me about Mrs H. 'She's a bit house proud and everything in the house is spotlessly clean. She locks up at 10.30 p.m. If anyone is not in then they will be locked out.'

After we had seen to the horses we all walked up to Mrs H.'s house. She was just as Darley had said. She was very straight-laced and watched us all wipe our feet as we came in the door then showed us where we would be sleeping.

A lad Darky asked me to keep an eye on was to share the same room as me. The room was actually the downstairs front room with a large bay window and two single beds in it. In the evening we went down to the Seven Stars pub in the village. It was a really good evening with Micky Fin, the Lambourn horsebox driver, playing the piano and nearly everyone singing along with him. Darley went back up to Mrs H.'s house early. The lad I was sharing the room with had got involved with a local girl so when it was time to go the lad came to me and said he was going to take the girl home and asked me if I would just let him in through the window. I told him not to be long. 'It's alright, I won't be,' he said, 'and I'll just tap on the window,' Off he went before I could say a word.

In the morning when I woke up the first thing I saw was this lad looking at me through the window. He was wet right through, his hair was flat on his head and the suit he was wearing was all crumpled. He looked as if he had been in a shower with all his clothes on. I went to the window and was going to let him in but when I looked at his feet I couldn't. He had mud all over his shoes and up his trouser legs. He must have walked up and down all night in the rain. The front garden looked like a herd of cows had run through it; the lovely flowers were broken and trodden into the ground. He started to shout, 'Let me in!' Darley heard him and came into our room, took one look at him through the window then turned and shot out of the front door. I could hear Darky calling the lad all the names under the sun. He told him to go to the stables and wash himself. He had to give some money to Mrs H. to help make good the mess in the front garden.

When I saw the lad again later I asked him if the girl was worth all the trouble. With a miserable look on his face he said, 'No'.

Clarence, the horsebox driver, looked him up and down and said, 'Any girl who had any sense would keep miles away from you. Look at you, your hair is a mess and you don't even know what size clothes to wear.' The lad's clothes had shrunk when they had dried out and his trouser legs ended just below his knees.

Joker

I can remember one evening stable when the Major was looking round the horses. He had a group of people with him. When they came near to my horse box I could hear a lot of laughing. Being in a joking mood I went up to the Major with my finger to my lips and all the group of people went quiet. The Major look at me and said, 'What is wrong?'

I replied that my horse had a terrible headache and could they be a bit quieter. They all stopped talking and looked at me for a moment then the Major burst out laughing and said, 'You're a real little joker, Alwin.'

I can remember another time when I was working with the yearlings. Jim and I were taking a yearling down to the lunging ring. Jim was leading the yearling and I was walking behind it. Just before we went by the Major's office window I got hold of the yearling's tail and pulled it right out straight, held on to it and frogmarched past the Major's office window. The Major looked up, his mouth opened wide and he came flying out of the office.

'What's wrong with him?' he asked.

'Oh, I'm just checking to see if he had got his hat on straight.' I was in the first place checking to see that the yearling had not got any hair caught in the cropper which he had on at the time. A cropper is put under a horse's tail to help keep the roller in place and the roller is a large padded garth. The Major smiled and shook his head. Later on when we came back in the Major came up to me and said, 'You took a bit of a chance with the yearling, he could have kicked you.'

'No,' I said, 'I always pull the yearlings' tails out straight when I groom them. It's my way of finding out what kind of a temperament they have before you get on them to ride. If they are hard to groom they sure are likely to be hard to ride.'

A lad called Reg looked after a horse two boxes away from my horse. Reg was a lovely person and treated his horses like children to the point of being too soft with them. He would put the straw just right and make it level, then he would ask the horse to move over so he could do the other side of the box. The old horse would drag his feet across the box and pull all the straw with him and make a right mess of it. Then to top it all he would do a dropping on top of it. I could hear Reg calling the horse a dirty so and so. Then out he would come rushing to get rid of the dropping before the Major arrived to see the horse. If by chance my horse had done a dropping too when I had finished doing him and I was also waiting for the Major, I would see Reg run up the yard· and round the corner with his muck sack to the muck hill. As soon as he was out of sight, I would pick up my horse dropping and put it in Reg's horsebox, right under his horse so it looked like he had just done it. Of course when Reg came back I could hear him calling his horse all sorts of names. I would go up to him sometimes the next day and ask him what was going on with his horse last night, just to get him going. Reg would say, 'He is a very good horse but I have never seen so much shit come from one horse.'

One night I was doing the same trick with the dropping but Reg must have run back from the muck hill. I heard him just in time so I walked out of his horsebox carrying the nest of droppings that I was going to leave.

'Reg, look what your horse did as soon as you went! I looked and saw that your horse had done a dropping so I picked it up to put in with my horse muck.'

'Oh, that was good of you,' said Reg.

'Does you horse always do it when you leave the box, Reg?'

'Yes,' said Reg.

'What a funny horse, he must be having you on, Reg.'

'No he isn't, he thinks he's going to be ridden out so he lightens his load,' said old Reg with a smile on his face, 'but he's a real good un!'

A couple of days later Reg said to me, 'Come and look at the mess my horse had made of his bedding.' I looked at it and what a mess it was in. I said, 'He sure had a big load to lighten this time.' I could not stop myself from laughing. 'Do you think your horse is just full of shit and nothing else?'

'Well, they say where there is muck there is money'.

'Well in that case your horse is going to make you a lot of money,' I said. The horse Reg looked after was a very very good horse call Sun Prince so you see there might be something in that saying.

Hard Lesson

It was a lovely summer day and in the afternoon the Major had asked three of us to help him bring in the hay bales that had been made in the paddock down bv the drive because it looked like it might rain. As we were putting the bales of hay onto the trailer a very smart car came along the drive and stopped by us.

Two young men got out of the car and walked up to the trailer. We all looked at them. They were dressed in what we would call their Sunday best, nice suit and collar and ties, shiny shoes.

The Major asked what they wanted. One of them said, 'We are trying to find a Major - ' but before the man could finish what he was going to say the Major said, 'Don't just stand there, can't you see we need some help.'

So the men started to throw up the bales of hay onto the trailer. As the pile of hay got higher it was harder for them to throw the bales, because we stacked them very high to get as much hay on this trailer as possible. I looked down at the two men struggling; they were sweating and their clothes were covered with hay and they had bits in their hair. They looked a very sorry sight indeed. When we had finished one of the men said, 'Can we see the Major now?'

The Major looked the man straight in the face and shouted, 'Of course you can't see the Major looking like that.' The man asked 'Can we call at the Major's house to say we came before we go?'

'You want to go knocking on my door. Well you can't, I am very busy,' said the Major, 'Give me a ring some time.' The two men looked at each other in disbelief with open mouths then walked away with their heads down. I never saw them again. The Major turned to me and said,

'Let that be a lesson to you - always try and test everything from a car to a horse to people to find out what they are made of.'

Another time the Major brought a young man up to the yard and introduced him to us. 'This is Peter,' said the Major, 'who would like to be an amateur jockey.'

The Major turned to me and said, 'You and Peter will come with me after breakfast.'

About 10 a.m. I was waiting outside the Major's house. Out came the Major shouting over his shoulder at Peter.

'Don't stand there all day, come on.' Into the Land-rover we got. I said nothing. Peter asked the Major where we were going. 'To see how good a pilot you are,' he answered.

'But I want to be a jockey,' Peter quickly replied.

The Major looked at Peter and said, 'How good a pilot is is a term used by the racing fraternity for a jockey. We are going to see a Miss Joy Bassett, a wonderful lady who knows more about horses than all of us.'

When we arrived the Major introduced Peter to Joy Bassett. I had already met her.

'Have you got the pony ready?' asked the Major.

'Yes,' said Miss Bassett and she went into the barn and brought out a lovely grey pony.

'Are the jumps up?' asked the Major.

'Yes,' said Joy. 'Don't you hurt this pony will you now?'

'Of course not, you silly ass,' shouted back the Major.

Peter looked a bit worried. The Major said to me, 'You show Peter how good a jumper this pony is first then Peter can show us how good he is.' Miss Bassett looked at me as I was about to jump up onto the pony and said, 'You will have to wash it down when you are finished.'

'Stop being such a silly ass, Joy, of course we will see to the pony,' said the Major.

'There's a lot of mud out in the ring and he is sure to get dirty,' said Joy.

The Major told me to just jump the pony round once and then pull up and give it to Peter. So off I went and the pony just jumped round and made it look easy without me doing anything but point him at the jumps. I gave him to Peter to do the same. Off went Peter, he pulled up after doing the same as I did and came over to the Major with a big smile on his face.

'Very good', said the Major, 'now I would like you to do it again but this time I would like you to fold your arms and let go of the reins when you jump the middle jump in the centre'.

Peter set off again and when he came to the middle jump he went to let go of the reins but at the last moment he kept hold of them. The Major shouted, 'What did I tell you to do? Now next time let go of the reins and fold your arms, then I will know how good a seat you have and balance'. Peter had lost his smile by now. 'Well go on, then,' shouted the Major, 'We haven't got all day,' So off went Peter with the Major shouting, 'Don't hang about!'

The pony was a bit geed up and had set off fast. The Major shouted at Peter as he came to the middle jump, 'Fold your arms!' The pony was really going by now. Peter dropped the reins and before he had time to fold his arms the pony took off and poor Peter went out the back door and landed in all the mud as he hit the ground; he rolled over so that one side of his face was covered in mud. What a sorry sight he was. The Major was laughing his head off. 'Now you have learnt one of the best lessons you can ever have - don't be bullied to do something against your better judgement'.

I really felt sorry for Peter but I must say he took it very well and burst out laughing. We spent a long time cleaning the pony and we mucked out his box too.

Miss Bassett and the Major checked that all that should be done for the pony was done, not that there was anything wrong with the pony.

A Long One Hour

Joy Bassett was a great character. One day she asked me if I could find someone to move some horses from one paddock to another - this would only take about an hour to do. I asked a good friend of mine, Donny, to help. I told him we had to go in Miss Joy Bassett's car, which was never anything to look forward to, so not to wear his Sunday best and we both laughed. Miss Joy Bassett's car had the seats covered with old bran sacks and she always took her dogs with her wherever she went. The smell of dogs in her car was overpowering. You could be sitting in the front talking to Miss Bassett and it would not be long before a big wet tongue from one of the dogs was licking you all over your face. When I looked round at Donny in the back of the car he had two of her dogs in his lap.

We arrived after about 25 minutes and caught the two horses. Miss Bassett told us to just follow her to the car. She held the door open and shouted in her manly voice to the dogs to get in. 'Come on,' she called to us, 'follow me.' So off we went along the road with Miss Bassett going along in front in her car.

After about 20 minutes, Donny asked me where we were going. 'I don't know,' I said. Miss Bassett kept going on and on. I was getting a bit annoyed because I had told Donny it would only take about an hour as Miss Bassett had said. After nearly an hour we came to the paddock and let the horses loose. When we got back Miss Bassett said to Donny, 'Come in, I'll give you a drink.' I went off because I had to see someone and of course I was late.

The next day I asked Donny if Miss Bassett had looked after him. Donny just laughed and said, 'I never in all my life met anyone like her before.'

'Did she give you a drink then?'

Donny smiled and said, 'She asked me if I would like money or whisky. I said I would like whisky, so she brought out a bottle which had about one inch of whisky in it, and said there you are then.'

'What did you say to her?' I asked.

'I was too shocked to say anything,' answered Donny with a little smile on his face.

I never asked anyone to do anything for her again.

Maggots

Joy Bassett used to go away to pony camp in Ireland for a month or so. Before she went she would have her horses turned out at a friend of hers. I can remember one time she came back from pony camp and asked me if I would go with her to see how her horses had done since she had been away. At that time she had a very bad foot, it looked very painful and she was walking around with a soft slipper on and with a walking stick but was still driving her car. When we arrived at this very big field where the horses were turned out there was quite a walk to the field.

Joy was in quite a lot of pain and her slipper was covered with mud. She leant on the gate and looked across the field and said in a joking way, 'Well, they are all stood up.' She asked me to go and check them over and catch one and bring it to her at the gate so she could see if they had put any condition on. I walked out into the field to catch one of the horses. As I got close I noticed two more horses that had been out of sight from the gate. By the time I had led the one horse with the other one following behind to the gate the two strange horses had come galloping up.

Joy was not very happy; the other horses were hostile to her two and to make things worse one of Joy's horses had a nasty cut down his near side shoulder. It looked horrible, with pus and maggots in the wound.

'That stupid gal,' she shouted, 'she has not even looked at these horses and I gave her the vet's telephone number in case of anything like this. I didn't give her permission to put any other horses out with mine.'

When we got home Joy had to have the doctor to see to her bad foot and could not go out. I did what I could with all her animals - not only did she breed horses and ponies but dogs, chickens and cage birds. David, a man who lived in the village and did some work for her, helped out. Miss Bassett not able to go out was like a tigress that had been penned in.

After a few days she asked me to go and check the two horses. When I knocked on the door of the person who owned the big field it flew open and the lady was so angry. She stormed at me, 'That Miss Bassett had a real cheek telling me off about her two horses, there is nothing wrong with them'. Having learnt the hard way I said nothing.

'I'll come with you and you can show me this terrible wound that Miss Bassett is shouting about'.

When we got to the field there were only Joy's two horses there - she had got her way. I was surprised to see only a pink mark on the horse's shoulder where the wound had been.

'Well, where is the wound that is so nasty it is going to make me sick to look at it?'

I showed her the pink mark

'Is that it? You mean to say that bit of pink with no hair on is what Miss Bassett is making all the fuss about!'

'Well, yes,' I said. If I had not seen how it looked before I would not have believed it. 'Joy said about yellow pus and maggots coming out of the wound?'

I said, 'Yes it looked horrible.'

The hair grew back within a month and you could not see anything at all, not a mark.

Lady Killer

One time I was going racing and had to stay over for the night. I was sharing a horsebox with three other horses. The lads who were travelling with the others horses were a mixed bunch, two head lads and two apprentices. Most of the talking was done by one of the apprentices who was a bit of a know-it-all. He asked one of the other apprentices what he thought of his girlfriend.

'She looks very nice, are you in love with her?' asked the apprentice.

'Yes, she is so pretty and bright.'

'Oh, is she?' said the horsebox driver. 'I expect she is like the rest of the women.'

'What do you mean by that?' asked the apprentice, a bit put out at the horsebox driver's remarks.

'She may be pretty and look very nice but if she wants to go to the toilet she will shit anywhere.'

'You are disgusting,' said the apprentice with a look of distaste on his face.

The box driver was laughing his head off.

The other apprentice spoke up and asked how many girlfriends have you got? The girl I saw you with last night was not the same girl you were with last week.'

'I have three girlfriends.'

'No wonder you look like John Jorrocks in Fizsick when you are riding out,' said one of the head lads.

We all laughed then the other head lad turned to the other apprentice and said to him, 'I don't know what you're laughing at, you look like a sack of shit tied in the middle, bumping up and down like a pea on a drum'.

When we arrived at the racecourse the box driver went off to find out where we could stay the night.

Sometime later he came back with a smile on his face. 'It's alright,' he said. 'But one of us will have to stay with the widow. We'll draw straws to see who is going to be the lucky one.'

'Knowing my luck,' said the box driver, 'I'll get the short straw.' It was the one who drew the long straw who was the lucky one to stay at the widow's house that night. How the box driver managed the draw is a mystery to me but I am sure he fiddled it somehow. I got a short straw, so did the box driver, then the apprentice with the girlfriend got the long straw. Straight away the driver said, 'I could have gambled that you would win.' He then turned and winked at me. The apprentice who won the draw kept asking the driver what the widow lady was like. He replied, 'All I know is that the fellow who I asked about staying the night somewhere said whoever stays the night at the widow's house will have a real good night and marvellous food.'

Early the next morning at the racecourse stables we met the apprentice who had stayed at the widow's house. He looked very cold and not at all happy. 'Well what was it like at the widow's?' I asked. Before the apprentice could answer the racecourse security stableman said, 'He's been here since eleven o'clock last night. I let him stay here with me.'

'What went wrong at the widow's?' we asked. He didn't say anything; he just looked at the ground with his head bent down.

'We took you right to her front door and watched you go in so what went wrong?'

He looked up with a tear in his eye and said, 'She tried to get hold of me.'

'What do you mean, she tried to get hold of you?'

'After I had supper with her I went to the bathroom and was in the middle of washing my face when she came up behind me and got hold of my balls and took my hand and put it between her legs, it was horrible!' cried the apprentice. 'I ran out of her house back here.'

We all could not stop laughing. One of the travelling head lads, still laughing said, 'And you are the one who is a lady killer with all the girlfriends!'

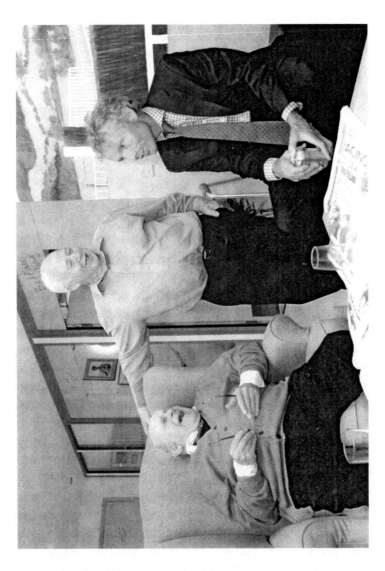

*John Lawrence "Lord Oaksey" left, the author and
fellow jockey John Francome at Oaksey House
Lambourne 2012*

Lucky Escape

In John Lawrence, "Lord Oaksey", I have always seen a wonderful sense of humour and fair play.

When working for Major Dennistoun, known as 'Ginger', I can remember during the bad weather of 1962-63, John Lawrence took Tony Perkins and myself in a Landrover with a snow sledge or toboggan in the back.

John took us to the top of Sycombe Hill. With so much snow on the road, we only just made it ·to the top. We walked across the gallops and schooling ground with John pulling this long sledge. The snow was very deep and the sledge went smoothly over it.

'Come on,' said John, 'we can all get on this sledge together.' We stood looking down into what looked like a deep canyon with high sides and at the bottom we could only see a kind of mist. We could not see very well but John Lawrence, being John Lawrence, was not put off by this and said 'come on Tony and you Bobby', so all three of us got onto the sledge and started to push it along over the snow with our feet. The sledge suddenly took off at a great speed. Tony Perkins was hanging onto John and I was hanging onto Tony at the back.

We went down the slope at a good speed that was thrilling to me, then we hit a very big bump in the ground. We all went flying into the air, laughing as we lay in the snow. No one was hurt, but the sledge was broken in two. We lay in the snow looking down the slope - a few yards away was a metal water trough which is still there to this day. John said 'how lucky we are to have hit the bump and not the metal drinking trough,' and just kept laughing. The next day John

Lawrence arrived at the stable yard with three brand new sledges.

Oaksey House Lambourne

Larry the Lamb who was a Ram

We had a yearling one year that was very nervous and would walk round and round in his box so the Major got a little lamb and put it in with the yearling to help settle it down. It worked so well the yearling could not keep his eyes off the lamb. When we fed him we would tie the lamb up just outside the box and give it some food too. The yearling would be alright as long as he could see the lamb eating just outside.

Jim called the lamb Larry and made a big fuss of it; he washed him and would cut his wool and look after him as if he was a racehorse. Some of the lads teased the lamb as it got bigger and made it run at them and butt them. They would encourage it by putting their hands together and running at him, he would charge forward with his head down and go smack at the upturned hands. Of course he was a young ram and this game went on nearly every day. He grew very big, and the horse he was with had settled down a lot.

One morning in the late spring when we were riding past the Major's house, I noticed some big lovely tulips all in wonderful colours. I turned to the Major and asked him if he had planted them. He said, 'Of course I did, they cost a lot of money and my wife is very pleased with them.'

Well somehow Larry the Lamb got loose, found his way down to the Major's garden and ate all the flowering tulips, not just one but all of them. The Major came storming up to the yard; his face was red with anger and he called for Jim and gave him a right bollocking for letting the ram loose. Jim was always on the ram's side and would not have a word said against him. He even said that one of the lads must have led him down to the garden.

Two days later Jim was bent over a bucket cleaning some stable rubbers when Larry the Lamb saw Jim's big behind bent over. He just could not resist the temptation and ran at Jim, hitting him full in the bottom - it was like a cannon going off. Jim went two yards up in the air and came down with a thump. The ram kept running at him, he ran back and then charged forward with his head down as Jim lay on the floor flat out and butted him again. I caught Larry and tied him up then went to Jim who was still on the floor. I helped him up; he was in a bad way, his face was all cut and the skin had come off his nose. Jim was over 60 years old. Some years ago a horse had kicked him in the face and he had lost an eye, so this attack really shook him up. Jim was taken to see a doctor and when he was away we took Larry the ram back to the farm, never to be seen again. The horse that he had been with was all right without him and seemed happy that he had gone. I am sure Larry used to eat most of the horse's hay.

The horse turned out to be a top class racehorse and won a lot of races.

Hard Riding Lesson

I would like to tell you about one of the most important things I learnt when I was an apprentice. One day the Major took me down to a paddock on a two year old filly. He led me to the paddock, opened the gate, shut it behind me then told me to trot the filly round in a figure of eight. As soon as I asked the filly to trot on she stuck her head between her front legs and bucked and dropped her shoulder, I went flying off.

The Major shouted, 'Catch her and get on again.' The filly was eating grass. I walked up to her, got hold of the reins and tried to get on but she would not stand still, so the Major came and gave me a leg up. He said, 'Go on, trot her on and do a figure of eight.' The filly did the same thing again and off I came. This went on for about seven times. I was so upset when the filly dropped me the seventh time that instead of going back to the Major for a leg up again I went up the paddock and just round the corner out of sight. I led the filly up to the paddock rails and let her eat grass. While she was eating I got a stick out of the hedge about three feet long with leaves on it. I could hear the Major shouting for me to come back. I put my feet on the second rail of the fence and very slowly got on the filly again. I sat there for a moment and she had her head down eating grass. When she had a big mouthful of grass I pulled her head up and got a good hold of the reins in one hand and with the other hand with the stick in it, I hit her as hard as I could. She shot off, bucking and kicking. I hit her again and sat well back. She went flying round the corner in the paddock and nearly knocked the Major over. We were going round the paddock at a good lick with the Major shouting, 'Stop, you bloody fool, you'll kill yourself!' I stopped the filly and made her stand still while the Major walked up to us. He looked at me and said, 'Trot on and do a figure of eight.' I asked the filly to move on and trot off and we went and did the figure of eight.

The Major said, 'Now do it again without the stick,' which I did. The filly kept twitching her ears to listen to my voice. I made her do everything right. The Major said that I had learnt a great lesson about how some horses will try and take advantage of you if you let them. I must have made some impression because the next day, when I was about to ride out, the Major put his hand in his pocket and pulled out two ten shilling notes. He said, 'You see these two notes, I want you to put one between your knees and the saddle so that they stay between your knees all the time when you are out at exercise. The head lad and I will make sure you keep them there all the time. If you lose them I will take it out of your wages'.

My wages were five shillings a week, twenty-five pence in today's money. It was very difficult. I was so glad to get back to the yard and get off the horse as soon as I could. The next morning the top of the inside of my thighs was so sore and my muscles ached. I had a job to walk with the pain. I was hoping the Major would not tell me to do it again. One of the lads said the Major was going away for a couple of days so I was glad, but not for long. The head lad gave me a leg up on to my first ride of the day then pulled out the two ten shilling notes. He said, 'The Major asked me to make sure you keep doing this all the time'.

After a while the ache wore off. It was not easy to do, I lost one note so I put the other note in my pocket and got off the horse to get the one I had lost; the head lad shouted at me. I found the note and took a long time trying to get back on the horse again. I managed by getting on a bit of a bank at the side of the road. Anyone who has done this knows it is a special knack. I became very good at it - one, two and I would be up on a horse's back.

When the Major came back from his holidays he said to me that the head lad told him I had been very good about keeping the ten shillings notes between my knees but he would find out how good I was. Now there was a horse in the yard that had a sore back and could not have a saddle put on him so the Major said I was to ride him out with just a folded blanket held on with a sursingle. The sursingle was a long strap that is used to keep a top exercise blanket on over the saddle. To my surprise I managed to sit there on the horse well and when we had to trot on I never moved my knees but rode as if I had a saddle on, no trouble. The next day the Major, who had been riding behind me, said, 'Right, we will do a hack canter up the five furlongs'.

I am sure he thought that I would not do it and I would be in trouble. He set off behind me; after we had gone for three furlongs he came up beside me and looked across. I just sat there with my hands down on the horse's neck and smiled back at him. The Major had come alongside me because he thought it would make my horse pull more and I would find it hard to hold him and stay on. But I had got very confident in my own horsemanship. I could not help but smile.

From then on the Major started to talk to me about the horses and I found that I was riding the better horses in the yard.

Miss Joy Bassett Being Mean

Another story about Joy Bassett. When she had her bad foot she would ask anyone she could to help do housework for her, like washing up and cleaning the house. I called in to see how she was this particular day, and a young girl was at the sink just about to wash up the dirty dishes. Joy and I were talking when all of a sudden she shouted at the young girl, 'What are you doing with that dish pad?'

'I'm going to wash the dishes with it.'

'No you don't, you wasteful girl', she retorted in a very loud voice. When Miss Bassett shouted you could hear her all over the village. 'Give it to me, girl!' she shouted so the young girl gave her the green dish pad upon which she cut it into four pieces and gave one very small piece about an inch square back to the girl telling her to make it last a long time and not to let it go down the drain, and not to take all day at the sink moon gazing. .Just after that I left.

On the way down the road I caught up with David. I asked him why he was not going to see Miss Bassett because she had said she was expecting him. He said that as he got near to her yard he heard her shouting so he turned round to go back home.

'I always do that if I hear her shouting'.

'What will you say when she asks you why you did not come?' 'I always say that I was not well. You see I get what is known as migraine or a bad headache,' he said and he laughed. Some years later I was talking about Miss Bassett to a friend of mine. I told him about the young girl getting into trouble with the washing up dish pad. When I got to the part where Miss Bassett cut the pad into four pieces he started to roar with laughter. I said I did not think it was funny, but he just kept laughing.

'What is it that is making you laugh so much?' I asked.

My friend said, 'Because I have seen my mother-in-law doing the same thing and when l asked my wife why she did it she told me that when she got to the last little bit it reminded her to buy another dish pad'. My friend said he had told his wife it was the height of meanness and it was not to remind her at all.

Concerning Miss Bassett being mean, sometimes I would take my son with me to see her. He liked to see the animals and would play with the puppy, a Jack Russell that Miss Bassett liked to breed. On this day there was only one puppy left and my son played with it on the lawn as I was talking to Miss Bassett. We went up to see her a week later and the same puppy was still there. My son spent all the time playing with it. As we stood watching them playing Miss Bassett turned to me and said, 'Your boy and that puppy are getting on well together, aren't they?'

'Yes,' I said.

'He'd better have the puppy then', said Miss Bassett.

My son was delighted and we took the puppy home. About ten days later Miss Bassett asked, 'How are your son and the puppy getting on?'

'Very well,' I said.

'Good,' she said, 'that will cost you £7 10s. for the dog.'

I didn't know what to say. £7 10s. was a lot of money to me then. Of course I paid her but I made sure that I was very careful when dealing with her after that.

It Was Worth the Effort

It is amazing how much time and effort people will put into a horse to make it win. I can remember we had a very good looking horse in the yard which could beat every other horse on the gallops but when it came to run in a race, even with blinkers fitted, he still did not put in much effort.

The Major came up with the idea that he would shut up the horse in a very large box and seal it so that there was no light. I watched the Major put the sticky tape round all the cracks in the stable door. 'Now he can't see a thing', he said. I looked the Major and asked, 'Who is going to go in to feed him and is he going out for exercise?'

'No, he's not going out until he goes to the races, and I am going to get up early in the mornings when it is still dark to feed him and muck him out with just a torch to see with'.

'Well if you ask me ... 'I started to say, but before I could finish the Major shouted, 'I am not asking you, I am telling you. No one but myself will go in to this horse until he runs and the bloody doors to this box will have two padlocks on and I will be the only one to have a key.'

He was right to keep it locked because he knew as soon as he had gone someone would go and open it up. He started to walk away when I said, 'Major, you have forgotten something'.

'What?' he snorted back.

'There's a small window right down the other end of the horsebox,' I told him.

'Damn!' said the Major, 'you're right. Get something to cover it from the outside'. So we covered it with some hardboard and taped it. 'How do you know there isn't a small hole he can stand and look through?' I asked.

'I'll go inside and you can seal up the door all the way round'.

So in goes the Major and I close the doors and bolt them, and put back the sealing tape. Just as I am putting the last piece of tape on the box the horse got frightened and started running round in the box.

The Major started to shout, 'Let me out! Let me out!'

I quietly opened the door at the bottom and out came the Major rolling on the floor. The horse was lively and tried to get out too but I managed to keep him in. It was a good job I did not open all the doors or he would have got away. The Major looked up at me as he sat on the floor, he was laughing. 'It is going to work.'

'What's so funny?' I asked.

'You are going to get up early with me to see to this horse in the mornings and at night when it's dark.' So that is how it was for about four days. As each day went by the horse became more jumpy. As soon as he heard us at the door he wanted to get out so we only opened the bottom of the stable door to get in to see to him. We had left a head collar on him so we could catch him.

The first thing was to get hold of him to stop him running round the box and knocking us over. I would go in with a bucket and a torch on top of the feed which was in the bucket, catch him, lead him up to the manger and put his feed in and tie him up to the ring on the wall with a long enough rope so he could reach his feed.

While he was eating I would muck him out and give him fresh hay and water. The Major would stand at the door and watch all the time. It was not easy to muck the horse out with just a torch to see by and when it came to let him loose he would run at the door to get out. I would be hanging onto the end of the rope on his head collar trying to stop him. As soon as the Major turned off the torch the horse would stop for a moment and I would dive through the bottom of the stable door, which the Major would quickly lock and seal up again.

When it came to the day of the race the Major gave me a special bridle to put on the horse, to load him into the horsebox to travel to the races. The horsebox came very early in the morning to take him to the races and we weren't sharing, we went on our own. The Major was there to see the horse loaded into the horsebox. He told the driver to back up right into the corner as near as he could and drop the ramp so the horse would come straight out and up the ramp and into the horsebox.

The Major and I got the horse ready to travel; we put big bandages on all his legs and a tail bandage, just using the light from the torch. The driver stood at the stable door watching. He asked 'What's wrong with the light?'

The Major shouted at him and said 'All you've got to do is to look after this lad and horse at the races. Now just you keep quiet.' We did load the horse successfully. It came out of the box like a rocket and straight up the ramp. As soon as he was in the Major and the driver lifted the ramp and shut it.

'Good,' said the Major and picked up some hardboard that he had ready with some tape. We taped up as much as we could to stop the horse seeing any light - he was in total darkness. The Major told the driver to let the horse out as near as possible to the stable door when we got to the racecourse. He told me to lock and tape the stable up and leave the horse with a muzzle on like we always did with a horse when it was loose in the racecourse stable before a race. The Major said he would come and see me to let me know what time to bring the horse across to the racecourse paddock.

He came to the racecourse stables a bit late on purpose to tell me to bring the horse to be saddled up for the race. It came out of the stable with its eyes sticking out of its head like organ stops. I had a job to keep him under control. It was a good job the Major had given me the right kind of bridle and chifney to help control him. The Major told me to follow him to a saddling box. He made sure no one else would use the box; it had a sign on the door, 'Vet Box only'.

The horse at first would not go in but the Major shouted at him and in he went. We were late going into the parade ring and when the jockey saw the horse he looked a bit worried but said nothing. When the Major gave him a leg up the horse leapt into the air and tried to get away from us. When I left to go down to the start I thought the horse was going to run away with the jockey. Somehow the jockey controlled him at the start; he was a top class hurdle jockey of that time. When the tape went up the horse shot off in front and was never overtaken. He won the race easily and was sold there and then. The jockey asked me what we had given the horse; I just smiled and said, 'nothing'.

Joking on the Phone

This anecdote is about coming back from the races.

An ex-national hunt jockey who had ridden the winner of the Grand National Steeple Chase at Aintree, Liverpool, some years previously was coming home with an owner who had offered him a lift.

On the way back the ex-national hunt jockey said to the owner that he would like to see a special TV programme which was on that night. If he could hurry he would be home in time to see it.

'All right,' said the owner, and for a little while he increased his speed. Then he slowed down to a snail's pace. The ex-jockey said, 'Can't you go a bit faster, I'll not be back in time to see the programme'.

'What time is it going to start?' asked the owner. The ex-jockey told him the time. 'That's OK then, you'll be back in time.' True enough, he was.

He got out the car saying, 'Thank you very much for getting me here in time. I'll come and see you tomorrow, goodnight.'

The owner drove his car slowly for about ten minutes until he came to a telephone box. He made a call then got back into his car and waited some five minutes or so. He went back to the telephone box again and made another call and then came back to his car laughing. He did it again in about five minutes and every following five minutes for up to about forty-five, - each time he came back to the car laughing more than the last time.

The ex-national hunt jockey came to see him the next day. At first they just talked about the day's racing. As casually as he could the owner asked the ex-jockey if the TV programme he had wanted to watch was good.

'How the bloody hell do I know!' shouted the ex-jockey. 'Some bloody Chinese take away kept ringing me up every five minutes talking rubbish down the phone.'

The owner could not stop himself from bursting out laughing.

This next thing that happened between the same owner and jockey was inspired by a television programme about practical jokes. The jockey invited the owner to his house to show him what he had done to his garden. When the owner arrived the ex-jockey showed him around the garden pointing out the new lawn and the water pond with a fountain. He was very pleased and proud of his house and garden. About a month later he went to see the owner and was in a right state. 'What ever is the matter?' asked the owner. 'You look like death warmed up.'

The jockey sat down in a chair and looked up at the owner and said, 'I am ruined.'

'Why?' asked the owner.

'A man came to my door with papers to say he and his men were coming that afternoon to clear all my garden for foundations for a factory to be built two feet from the wall of my house. Of course I told him to f… off but he showed me the papers and said a solicitor was on his way to explain it all to me and would be there in a few minutes. The solicitor came with more papers. I read them then I telephoned my own solicitor. My solicitor said he had been trying to tell me but had not been able to contact me and there was nothing I could do about it.'

'So what happened?' the owner asked.

'The bloody bulldozers came and bulldozed the whole garden flat within an hour. They didn't try to save the flowers or anything.'

The owner could see that the joke had gone too far.

He said to the jockey, 'You'd better stay here for a few days while I make a few phone calls and see what can be done.'

The next day the jockey telephoned his solicitor again but could not get to talk to him because his secretary said he was not in the office. After about four days the ex-jockey told the owner he'd better go and see if he still had a house to go home to. When he arrived back home he could not believe his eyes. The whole garden had been put back as it was with a big water garden and a wonderful new lawn; even the house had been painted. There was a letter for him from his solicitor saying someone had got the wrong address and he hoped the cheque endorsed would be compensation for the inconvenience. This is a true story as far as I can remember it told to me. Of course I do know the name of the ex-jockey and the owner.

Head On

Greendown Gallops are by the ridge that goes along the Downs from Streetly to well past White Horse Hill, the ancient fort, where the White Horse is cut into the turf. With the white chalk it is easy to see. In the middle of Greendown Gallops there is a group of trees known as the Fifteen Trees. These can be seen as a landmark and stand out on the skyline as you approach from Oxford to Wantage.

To go onto the Gallops you pass through the gate to the left of the Fifteen Trees as you look at them from the Ridgeway. The other gate onto the Gallops is to the right. You cannot see both gates at the same time because the Fifteen Trees stand at the top of a hill.

When we went onto the Gallops we would hack straight down away from the gate at the right, past the schooling ground then stop at the edge of a sharp dip in the ground. We would walk down the dip to the T-junction then turn left to the start of the Gallop. Normally this Gallop goes past Greendown Farm and towards the gate on the right of Fifteen Trees. You may by this time be thinking this rather uninteresting but it will all make sense in the end. If you were one of the lads who was riding up on the Gallops with Captain Tim Forster you would remember one particular morning very well.

That morning I had been down to ride a two year old that was a bit of a problem, he had a mind of his own. He would do silly things like suddenly running across the road and up a bank or trying to rub you off him into the bushes. It was the first time we had taken him up to Greendown Gallops. There were two older horses to give us a lead plus the two year old I was riding and one other two year old.

The Major came up to the Greendown Gallops in his Landrover to open the gate. We walked onto the Gallops and the Major told us what to do. We had to hack down to the dip and then turn round and come back towards him, go past him round the bend and on up towards the Fifteen Trees and to go at a good speed. He told me to put my horse right by the inside fence behind the two older horses and have the other two year old on my outside. If the horse was going well and enjoying himself I had to let him run on towards the Fifteen Trees after we had gone round the bend and were going straight.

The two year old I was riding had been quite good all the way up to the Gallops. We all cantered down towards the dip stop, walked and then turned in on to the Gallop with the older horses just in front. We all set off at the same time. I was tight up against the fence, the other two year old was outside me and we went at a really good pace. I felt the two year old I was on going well within himself and I sat there with a double handful. I was just thinking how well we were going and that he could be a really good horse when, as we went to turn round the bend and up towards the Fifteen Trees, the two year old that had been outside me dropped back and my horse went straight towards the gate we had come through onto the Gallops. We nearly knocked the Major over. I did all I could to make my horse go round the bend but we hit the ridgeway fence with a big bang. I went through the air and landed on the other side of the ridgeway near the opposite fence. I jumped to my feet, running towards the Major, who had got into his Landrover and was driving it through the gate towards me. As I went to get into the car, I noticed more horses, - some had no lads riding them. I could see two horses running loose up the ridgeway towards Gramps Hill, the road out of Letcombe Bassett. I got into the Landrover, the Major locked the gate onto the Gallops then got in beside me and asked if I was alright. It was the first time I had given any thought to having hurt myself. I looked down at my jodhpur boot which had a small cut in the ankle elastic but could feel no pain. The Major said, 'You looked like a flying trapeze act from a circus,' and what a circus it turned out to be. He drove up the ridgeway toward the top of Gramps Hill.

'Whose horses were they that were on the Gallops the same time as us?' I asked.

'Captain Tim Foster's,' the Major said, 'and he is not a very happy man because as our horses went round the bend and up towards the Fifteen Trees, Captain Forster's horses came over the hill on the same Gallops. You hit the fence with a loud bang and three of his horses got loose.'

We caught up to the string of horses walking up the ridgeway. Captain Foster was riding his hack alongside one of the Major's horses ridden by John Lawrence (later Lord Oaksey). The Captain was shouting at him and calling him all the names he could think of, from an overgrown hairy monkey to a meaningless, hopeless ·individual.

The Major turned to me with a smile on his face and said, 'Captain Foster has gone too far this time', and we both burst out laughing. We were still laughing when the Major put his head out of the Landrover.

'What are you laughing at, Ginger?'

The Major said, 'It looks to me that the way you are bouncing up and down on that horse you could be in pain.'

'Bloody pain!' shouted Captain Foster. 'I've got three horses loose running all over the Downs and you say I look as if I am in pain.'

'Well, these things do happen in racing,' said Lord Oaksey in his well educated voice. Off went Captain Foster cursing at the top of his voice.

The two year old that I had been riding went all the way back to the stable yard and only had a small cut on his foreleg, just a red line, about five inches long. By evening stable time the two year old had gone out of the yard and I never heard of him again.

The Major told me that you can come across a horse like that which is a complete nuisance because it will always end up hurting someone and upset the other horses in the yard. Because they give you the impression they could be a good racehorse you are tempted to keep trying with them but it is never worth it. This two year old had already been gelded so there was nothing more you could do for him. I have seen many unruly horses change after gelding but it does not always happen.

The first six months that I went into racing, the National Hunt jockey who rode for the yard in which I worked as apprentice had broken his leg in a bad fall in a race and was hobbling around on crutches. I was surprised when he came up to me and invited me to his wedding and reception afterwards. It was the first time that I had been to a wedding; I was only fifteen and a half years old then.

When the big day came, Joe, an ex-army batman, took the lads and me to the wedding in a big shooting-brake type of a car. There were about eight of us and we sang in the car as we went from the church to the village hall for the reception. The weather was one of those days when it was sunny without being too hot. The best man stood up and gave a speech, it went something like this: 'I am sure you will all agree that it is a sad thing to see the groom with his leg in plaster. We hope it will not be too long before he is riding winners again, at least we all know he will be riding an odds on winner tonight.' Everyone in the hall burst out laughing.

The groom looked very embarrassed and his pretty bride went red in the face and looked down at the table in front of her. After the dinner when the wedding cake had been cut and more people had made speeches, the tables were moved and the chairs put round the walls of the hall and a dance band played. The lads sat down one side of the hall and the girls sat on the other side. Some of the older people got up and danced; the young girls looked across at us and we looked at them. None of us looked like we would get up and dance so off to the bar we went. I only had orange juice to drink, but the others were drinking all sorts of stuff. Then we went back to the seats and looked across at the girls on the other side of the hall. I asked the lad next to me if he was going to dance or could he dance. 'Of course I can dance,' he said.

'Well why don't you go and ask one of the girls to dance with you then?' I said.

'Alright, I will,' and up he jumped. I think it was because he'd had a bit to drink that gave him the courage to go across the hall to where the girls sat.

A lad next to me said, 'Why don't you go and ask a girl to dance too?' I told him I couldn't dance and it was the first dance I had been to. The lad that had gone across the hall didn't look as if he was having any luck, he went along the row of about six girls then he came to a big looking girl. She got up and danced with him 'The lad next to me said, 'Good God, what a sight! Did you ever see anything like it! I've never ever seen a big ass like that, she would have to turn sideways to get through a barn door.'

After the dance had finished the lad came back and sat down by us again with a big grin on his face. The other turned to him and said, 'You don't care what you pick up, do you?'

'What do you mean?'

'Well, you don't know where that girl has been, do you? You could catch anything you know and if you got her really worked up and she got hold of you she would crush you to death.'

We all started to laugh and the lad said, 'Come on then, let's see some of you get up and dance.'

A couple of them did get up and went straight up to the bar but one lad went across and asked a girl and she got up and danced with him. When it was getting late Joe asked me to go and find out where the lads had got to. I went outside to try and find them. It was a wonderful summer evening, the moon was bright and I could see quite well. I heard someone say, 'Whoa, whoa, stand still.' I turned a corner and looked down a short lane. At the end was a gate that led into a grass field, and two of the lads were inside the field. One of them had hold of a young cow which had a head collar on. The cow kept going round and round and the other lad was trying to get close to it. The one holding the cow said to the other, 'Come on, I'll give you a leg up, come on, you told me you could ride anything.' He bent his leg and the other lad gave him a lift up on to the cow's back. Immediately the cow took off across the field bucking and kicking. The lad only stayed on its back for a short way then fell off. He sat on the ground in the grass laughing and rolling over; his mate was laughing too as he went and helped him up. He got up off the ground singing, 'The cow jumped over the moon'.

I told them Joe was trying to get everyone together to take them back so the three of us walked back towards the hall. As we got near the hall two of the girls came running from the back of the hall laughing.

We stopped them and ask if they had seen any of the lads. The girls just pointed to the back of the hall and burst out laughing again. We went round to the back of the hall and there, laid out on the floor, gone to the world, was one of the lads, his trousers pulled down round his ankles and his underpants down below his knees - a big red ribbon tied round his private parts. One of the lads looked at me and said, 'Let this be a lesson to you, young 'un, women can be just as mischievous as men. They may look innocent and sweet. But if one of them had a mind to they will seduce you and there's not a lot you can do about it when it happens.'

Eventually we gathered up most of the lads, but we couldn't find one of them. I told Joe, who was by this time himself well on the way to being drunk - he was red in the face from all the whisky he had been drinking. 'I'll give him ten more minutes then we'll go, but first I must eat some more sandwiches to soak up the booze.'

After another fifteen minutes Joe said, 'That's it, we'll go without them.' So off we went. Joe drove very slowly and he went from one side of the road to the other. We dropped off some of the lads in the village then went up to the yard. At the back of the stables stood a bungalow with a thatched roof, the ground in front sloped down to the back of the stables and there was a big area of tarmac you could turn a large horsebox in.

We pulled George out of the shooting-brake and he leant against the side of the car. I asked him if he was alright. He looked down at me, pointed his finger and said, 'Alright, I'll show you who is alright,' and took two steps up the slope towards the bungalow. Joe told me to get back into the car, we still had Sean to get home. In I got and as Joe was turning the car round in front of the bungalow we could see George on his hands and knees. Joe stopped the car, and I got out. 'Are you OK, George?' I asked.

George replied, 'I'm alright, it's that bloody horse there with his big ass in the way. He got up and pointed to the chestnut tree that was by the path close to the bungalow wall. 'I'll get by that bastard this time, even with that bloody big tail he had sticking out.' He straightened himself up and made a run past the tree and out of sight. Joe called me to get back into the car and leave George, saying he would be ok. I was a bit worried about him but Joe kept saying, 'Come on! Come on!' so I did.

We arrived at the old Anvil pub which was not far from the Sparrow Pub. The Anvil was not a public house anymore, it had been changed into a house. Joe stopped the car a good twenty yards from the house and whispered to me to keep quiet. He said he would go and see if Sean's wife was still up. In a few moments he came back and said, 'It's all right, the light in the kitchen is on and the door is unlocked'. We tried to wake Sean up but he was fast asleep in the back of the car.

We couldn't rouse him so we dragged him out of the car. I couldn't lift him nor could Joe, we had to drag him all the way from the car to the kitchen and as we got him through the door of the kitchen he started to sing out loud, 'Danny Boy'. We heard his wife come running down the stairs. Joe and I just looked at each other then turned and ran back to the car, leaving Sean singing away on the kitchen floor.

The next day, Sunday, the day after the wedding, we found George still unconscious in the hedge at the back of the bungalow. He was oblivious to all that was going on. When we woke him up he had a terrible headache and said he couldn't remember a thing.

'No, I expect you don't, but I am sure you must remember that you proposed to the widow Evan don't you?' said one of the lads.

'What do you mean?' said George.

'Well, it's not for me to say, George, but I have never seen you like that before'.

'Like what?' asked George.

'You kept asking widow Evan for every dance and you really had her going, your hands were all over her'.

'What do you mean?' shouted George.

'Well, I did hear her say what wonderful hands you have, George, and oh, do that again, George, it feels so nice!' All the time the lad was talking to George he kept a straight face and looked him in the eye.

George shook his head and said, 'No, this can't be true.'

The other lad said, 'Well, George, of course it could be the making of you,' and as he said it patted him on the back.

'No, it's not true!' shouted George.

'Well go and ask Darky if it's true or not if you're not going to take my word for it.'

'I will', said George.

'Come here, Darky, and tell George about him and the widow Evan at the wedding,' and he winked at him. 'I just told George it could be the making of him.'

'Oh, of course, I agree, it could well be the ideal thing for you, George,' said Darky. (Darky didn't know what he was supposed to be talking about).

'Do you mean that you heard me propose to Mrs Evan?' George asked Darky.

Darky thought for a moment then said as concerned as he could, 'Yes, George, you made Mrs Evan smile and look up into your eyes, it was very romantic.'

'Stop all this!' shouted George, 'I'll go and see Mrs Evan myself.'

'I should take a nice bunch of flowers with you George. All the ladies like it said with flowers!'

The lad we hadn't been able to find after the wedding had lost his shoes, socks, trousers and underpants and had been arrested for causing a disturbance and walking around in an indecent manner. His clothes were found hanging on a spinster's washing line, and, of course, he was in for a lot of leg pulling. One of the older lads looked at him, looked down at his feet then up to his head, smiled and said, 'Who would have thought you of all people could be the one to stay the night with the spinster, and all night too!'

'No! I did not!' said the lad with a startled look on his face.

'Well we hear that the village copper had to have reinforcements to get you under control and put you in a cell. I mean look at you, you of all the lads.'

'I can't remember any of it,' said the young lad.

"TAXIDERMIST" Jockey JOHN LAWRENCE

Boldboy

I have been lucky to have worked with many brilliant horses such as Brigadier Gerard, Sun Prince, Busting and more. Boldboy was the horse that I will always think of and may be one of the best. Sir Gordon Richards, the marvel ex-flat jockey, at this time was racing manager for Lady Beaverbrook. He had gone to Ireland and bought a yearling for £13,000 on Lady Beaverbrook's behalf, which she named Boldboy.

I was asked to stay up late and be ready to see the yearling as they arrived from Ireland. At that time I was employed in the yearling yard. There were four or five lads who worked all day in the yard breaking the yearlings in. We were not allowed to go into the main yard in case the yearlings had brought in any coughing or bugs with them, it was a precaution against infections like ringworm.

The horsebox with the yearlings arrived at about 11.30 p.m. The driver told us about the yearling that would be coming out of the horsebox last. 'A good job they put this one in first, he had been kicking all the time and has a cut under his chin.' I was the one to bring this yearling out of the horsebox and of course it was Boldboy. When I led him out he walked off the ramp, stood for a moment and looked around, then lifted his head and arched his neck and seemed to lift himself up to his full height. When you led him he would try to lead you and his feet floated over the ground. When you lead some horses you feel that they are not interested in where they are going and you have more or less to drag them.

I led Boldboy into his box, tied him up, checked him over and put some treatment on his cut chin. He let me do the cut on his chin, nothing else was wrong with him.

I was impressed with the size of his quarters and the whole look of him. Next morning when I met the head lad he asked me how the yearlings were. I said OK and that I would like to look after Boldboy.

The head lad said he would put my name by his.

'Why do you want to do that yearling?' he asked. 'He only cost £13,000, Lady Beaverbrook has spent a lot more on some of the other yearlings.' I just smiled at him.

Because of the scratch on Boldboy's chin we could not put a bridle on him to lunge him in the sand ring so he was led out for a couple of days. He was getting a bit fresh on the second day so Jim Foggarty and I made a sponge pad to go on the kaverson and fit under Boldboy's chin so it would not hurt him, and we could start to lunge him in the sand ring and break him in to be ridden. Jim and I got Boldboy going round both ways, to the right and left, and put a lunge rein round him so that we could drive him from behind. We took him to the starting gates and led him through with the lunge rein each side of him with one of us walking behind. We did this with all the yearlings. Boldboy was no trouble.

Jim Foggarty was a very good man working with yearlings and when he saw how Boldboy moved round on the lunge rein he said, 'Bejesus, he's a fine horse and maybe the best to come out of Ireland this year.'

Little did we both know what hard work it would be to break him in. When we put the roller on him he stood quite still, Jim kept talking to him all the time as he tightened up the roller garth one hole at a time, very carefully. I stood at Boldboy's head with both lunge reins in my hands ready in case he tried to jump away. Jim stepped back and I let some of the lunge rein out. Boldboy stood for a second then he jumped into the air and roared like a lion. That was only the second horse that I had heard make that noise. The other horse was Partlet, I will tell you about him later on. Boldboy put his head down between his two front legs and bucked and kicked. We had to keep him moving forward or he might have come right over into a heap. After five minutes he was still fighting and he kept up this rodeo display for a long time. The Major came and watched Jim and I trying to steady him down. He must have heard the big roar the yearling had made, to bring him out of his office.

At last we got Boldboy to stop. He was sweating and his eyes looked like the Devil himself had gone into them. He would not let us touch him for a long time. We managed at last to remove the roller from him but when we went to take off his boots from his front legs he would not let us go near. He struck out with his leg and went down on his knees. Jim looked at me with sweat running down his face. I was sweating too, the sweat was going down my back and we both were blowing a bit. Jim wiped away some of the sweat from his face with his hand and said to me, as we looked at Boldboy blowing and snorting like a bad tempered bull, 'I never had a horse beat me yet and if he thinks he can beat us he's wrong.'

To get the boots off we put a lunge rein around him and pulled his front legs wide apart. Of course the horse was tired by now and so were Jim and I. It is very hard work running round in soft sand when you are concentrating all the time. Boldboy stood now with his front legs wide apart with Jim holding the lunge rein. I went up and took off the boots; we led him back to the yearling yard and washed him down then I walked him around for a long time to make sure he was alright.

Jim and I agreed to take Boldboy out last of the yearlings because of the time it was going to take to break him in. We used to take him out in the afternoon and slowly he got to accept the roller, then we put a saddle on him. It took longer than usual. The day came when Jim and I decided that I should lie across Boldboy's back on the saddle after we had given him a good lunging round in the sand ring. Jim gave me a leg up and I put myself slowly down across the saddle with my stomach on the seat straight away

Boldboy reared up and was walking on his hind legs round the sand ring. I stayed across his back hanging onto the saddle. After he had gone round rearing up and down Jim made him stand still and I slid off. We did the same thing the next day and I managed to stay across Boldboy's back without putting my legs each side of him but my ribs were sore by now.

Buster Haslem, the travelling head lad, came and stood by the sand ring and watched us working the yearling. He shook his head and said that Mr B. van Cutsem had a yearling with similar breeding and they never did break it in. Jim's quick reply was to say, 'and who is saying we won't be after breaking this wonderful horse in?' At the same time he gave Boldboy a pat on the neck and softly pulled his ears. Buster Haslem walked away shaking his head. This made Jim and I more determined to get the better of Boldboy.

Jim came up with the idea that the only way to get the horse to accept being ridden was to take him into the cover ride and to leg me straight into the saddle with my legs both sides. Jim would lead him round with a lunge rein so that he could slip it off him if everything was going all right. The cover ride is a round track with built up sides and a roof over it, wide enough to ride four horses alongside each other. There were radio loud speakers so that music could be played. It was big and very well built, with a room on the side next to the big entrance doors. This room was made so that the Queen and other owners could go in there and watch the horses go round. The cover ride was used every day. All the horses would go in first thing after the head lads had legged everyone up. The Major would watch each horse and lad as they approached the cover ride. He would stand by the big double doors at the entrance and sometimes shout at an apprentice to sit up straight, and keep his heels down. He would also check some of the horses' girths. When all the horses were inside, the head lad and the Major would get on their hacks and watch. The Major would shout for everyone to trot the horses on round the cover ride; he always did this so that he could see if they were trotting round sound and not lame as they went past him. The Major looked at his watch and commented to the head lad how long it took to get all the horses out and into the cover ride. He always checked on the yearlings and asked lots of questions on how each yearling was coming along. Most afternoons he was in his office but he would sometimes come and watch the yearlings being lunged. He never missed anything, even the smallest detail like a strap on a bridle not put on properly. This is what I think made him such a great trainer. He spent all the time he could at the stable yard and he always listened to you even if he did not agree.

We took Boldboy into the cover ride and closed the big entrance door behind us; just in case he did get loose he could not get out. When we were inside Jim gave me a leg up The horse reared up and kicked but he went forward, which is a good thing, and he looked back at me on his back. We went round the cover ride once. Jim made Boldboy stand still and I slowly got off his back. I can still see Jim looking up at Boldboy's face and quietly talking to him, 'You are some sort of horse and I'll shall be after telling ye now, as sure as God makes little apples, me Boldboy you will be as good a Christian to ride that there ever was, to be sure.'

We did the same thing the next day and Boldboy looked round at me as I was legged up onto his back with a hard look in his eyes as if to say, 'So you like to get on my back, well I'll show you.' Then up on his hind legs he would go, then come down, walk a few strides then he would rear up again. He did this all the way round the cover ride. When Jim stopped him and I got off his back, Jim said with a smile on his face, 'he didn't try and throw you off today.'

I think the thing that helped with Boldboy was when he did rear up I never pulled on the reins or said anything that was hard. I kept my hands down by my knees, close to the saddle flaps.

The next day I asked Jim to slip the lunge rein off so that we could see what he would do. As we got to the first bend in the cover ride Jim let the rein slip slowly away. Boldboy was dancing about a bit and had reared up but did not jump and kick so much. He was a bit surprised when Jim stopped so I asked him to trot on; his ears twitched backwards and forwards and he trotted on. I slowly put my feet into the stirrups and we trotted round, all the time I kept talking to him. Jim stood in the middle of the cover ride as we came round the bend with a big smile on his face. I pulled Boldboy up and gave him a pat on the neck. Jim suggested I go round once more on my own, just to see if the horse would try and kick me off or refuse in some way. Boldboy was good.

The next day we did the same thing and I said to Jim that I would like to ride him in the paddock on my own and he could watch at the gate. I went into the paddock with Boldboy and straight away he got hold of the bit. I hacked him round in figures of eight then I rode him up to the gate to Jim. Jim looked pleased and said, 'I'll lead you both through the starting stalls.' Boldboy walked straight through with no trouble at all. The rest of the week I rode Boldboy in the paddock and Jim would walk over to the starting stalls and watch us go through them. I said to Jim as he stood at the starting stalls that I would like to see if Boldboy would spring out of the stalls and really like to go. When .Jim opened the stalls we shot out like a rocket and the feeling of power behind the saddle was fantastic. I had a hard job to pull him up and he gave a squeal of delight. What a thrill to be on such a good horse. I made a lot of fuss of him with a pat on his neck.

At evening stable time Boldboy had a bad habit of pulling on the ring on the wall when he was tied up and would break the string on the ring, which was not very strong. This was in case a horse suddenly pulled back on the head collar the tie would break. Because Boldboy made a bad habit of this he was tied up with stronger string. Well, he ended up pulling the plank of wood fourteen feet with the ring he was tied up to out of the wall, and he went flying around his box with the plank of wood hanging from his head collar making a hell of a noise. We opened the door to his box and trapped the plank in the door. We jammed the plank there for a few minutes then I squeezed through the door and cut the tie on the head collar. The plank fell away and we pushed it out into the yard. Boldboy had a very nasty cut on his near side quarters made by the large nail sticking out of the plank.

Mr Charles Franks, the vet, came to see him and said, 'Just a few stitches and you won't see a thing.' He went for his medical kit. I put a head collar and a bridle on Boldboy to hold him for the vet who said, 'To be on the safe side I'll give him an injection to make him sleepy.' We waited about fifteen minutes for the injection to work. Charles Franks looked at Boldlboy's eyes and said, 'He looks as if he will go to sleep.' He got the needle and thread, closed the box door as he came in and put the catch on. Just as he went to put the needle into Boldboy's quarters to stitch it up the yearling kicked out with so much force the door was kicked open and the catch on the door was completely broken. Charles Franks went as white as a sheet. 'Well,' he said, 'it's a good job he missed me or he would have made a right mess of his OR my good looks!' and laughed. The vet went to his medical bag and came back with a bottle and cotton wool wad, and said to me, 'You know this horse better than anyone, so if you can let this antiseptic oil run down into the cut it will help to keep the wound clean'.

A few days later Lady Beaverbrook, the owner, came to look at her horses. When she came to Boldboy and saw the cut on his quarters she cried out, 'Major, what have you done with my best horse?'

The Major replied that the horse was highly strung and the wound was self inflicted; it would heal up and never be noticed. The cut did heal up all right, and you could hardly see it.

However Boldboy got up to more mischief when he started to do more work on the Gallop. He became more excited in his box. He was a good ride once we had broken him in and it was only when he was in his box that he would play around. One morning when I was getting him ready to go out for exercise I noticed how swollen his knees were. The Major said that maybe I had put his knee boots on too tight but I had been putting knee boots and bandages on horses for years and had never seen anything like that. When I went to tie him up at evening stable time I noticed a small cut on the side of his knee and blood on his mouth. Also there were horse shoe marks on the walls of the box and some of the wood panels were broken. I checked Boldboy's shoes and sure enough he had moved them. I went and fetched David the Farrier to look at the mess that he had made of his hind shoes. David re-shoed Boldboy, looked at the walls and said, 'If he carries on kicking the walls like that he will ruin his feet and kick his way into the next box.'

When the Major did his evening inspection and came to look at Boldboy, the first thing he said was 'What a mess he has made of the wooden walls!' He looked really annoyed. I told him that David the Farrier had had to re-shoe Boldboy.

'He did, did he?' said the Major. 'Well he'd better come and take them off again because if he keeps them on he will be kicking his way out of his box. Maybe with no shoes on he won't do so much damage. We'll keep him off the roads so that he doesn't get sore until we have made his box safe and sound. I have an idea that will help to stop him'. As the Major went to leave the box he raised his arm in a threatening way and shook his fist at Boldboy, saying, 'You're a monkey!'

Before the Major had finished what he was saying Boldboy flowed back on his head collar and kicked out before I could stop him. He just brushed the Major's trousers at the top of his thigh with his near hind foot. He jumped back with a shocked look on his face. It was the first time I had seen Boldboy try to hurt someone.

In the morning the builders came; they brought wooden railway sleepers with them and when Boldboy was out at exercise they began digging up the floor of the box. They made a two foot deep trench round the sides of the box and put concrete sleepers into the trench, up on their ends right round the box. Then a fish net was put right across the box about four inches above Boldboy's ears where he stood normally. This net was to stop him from rearing up; it worked and the railway sleepers worked too. The workmen put a thick steel plate all over the inside of the door. I thought this would help to keep him quiet.

The Major never liked anyone to do anything during the racing season in the yard in the afternoon. Let the horses rest, was the Major's saying, then he could see at evening stable how they really were. I was wondering if Boldboy was alright. As I came down to the stable yard I could hear a noise coming from his box so I very quietly crept up and looked through a crack in the door and watched. He was biting his knee, holding the skin in his teeth and running backwards and he was sweating. I went and found Buster Haslem who was in his racing tack room. I asked him to come and watch and I told him not to make a noise or Boldboy would stop. Buster came and watched Boldboy for a few minutes then the horse suddenly stopped and flared his nostrils.

'That's it,' I said to Buster.

'What do you mean?' asked Buster.

'Well, he has smelt us now.'

I went into Boldboy's box, tied him up and took off his rug. Buster looked at him and said he would get him a cooler rug and take his other rug to be washed.

When he came back with the cooler rug, I put it on Boldboy and then a bridle and led him out around the yard to settle him. Buster was watching us all the time.

'Does anyone else get on with Boldboy the same as you?'

'Yes,' I said, 'Jim Foggarty and Jack McCormack.'

Jack McCormack was a top apprentice when he was a flat jockey and was travelling head lad for Sir Gordon Richards when he was training. Jack McCormack would whistle as he went round the yard. I think Boldboy liked Jack because he always had something in his pocket to give him, a carrot or a polo mint.

The Major had a metal bar put in Boldboy's box right across, the same height as the ring. There was a long rein attached to his head collar, at the other end of the rein was a wooden ball. The rein was put behind the metal bar and the wooden ball attached to the end, this stopped him from running round in his box; of course the rein was long enough so that he could lie down. Because Boldboy was not letting off steam in his box he was more lively out at exercise. He was also showing how good he was on the Gallops. One day the Major was putting him through the starting stalls with some other two year olds but unfortunately Boldboy had a light lad on him who I would not have let ride my wife's bike. Boldboy took a strong dislike to the lad and reared up and threw him off. That was the worse thing that could have happened; it became a big game for Boldboy.

When he went to Ascot for his first race as a two year old, Lester Piggott rode him. The race had some of the very best two year olds running in it. When Lester Piggott was put up onto Boldboy I led them around the paddock. Before I led them out on to the racecourse to go down to the start, Lester Piggott looked down at me and said, 'The Major said that this horse may be a bit funny about the starting stall'. I replied, 'If you let Boldboy think there is anything odd about going into the starting stall he will play you up for a game and if you try and be on him he will fight you back.'

He ran a great race; he came fourth, beaten just over a length by the winner. The horse that won the race was never beaten in all his races and retired to stud unbeaten; its name was Sandford Lad, trained by Captain Ryan Price at Findon. I ran out on to the racecourse to lead Boldboy back into the fourth place unsaddling enclosure, but he went all the way down to Swindle Bottom before Lester Piggott could pull him up. When I did meet them coming back, Lester Piggott looked at me with a little grin on his face and said, 'This is the best two year old I have ridden this year. We should have won but I didn't want to be hard on him first on a racecourse.' He was very concerned in case Boldboy had sore shins because the going on the racecourse was hard. He went on to say that when I got Boldboy back to the stable yard I should put some ice pack on his front legs, which Buster Haslam and I did just in case he was sore. He was OK the next day and showed no signs of being sore.

As soon as I led them off the racecourse Lester Piggott never said another word. Even when the Major was asking him about Boldboy, he just took his saddle off and went straight to the weigh in. The Major asked me what the jockey had been talking about. I said, 'You'll never believe it but he said Boldboy was the best two year old he had ridden this year.'

Boldboy was to run next at Newbury. I thought that we could have a double that day with a horse called Donella and Boldboy. When Boldboy arrived at Newbury he was very excited. He was rearing up and jumping and kicking, I had a hard job keeping hold of him. I led him quickly into the racecourse stable and put a muzzle on him, then I went to the toilet. I was only gone for a few minutes but when I came back to him he was kicking at the brick walls and had moved his racing plates so I sent someone to get a farrier to replate him. The farrier was very good and Boldboy really liked him. He was so lit up we took him into a box to saddle him up. When Joe Mercer the jockey was legged up onto Boldboy in the paddock he was really playing up, jumping and kicking with excitement. I said to Joe, 'Don't try and fight him or he will get worse with you.'

'No he won't', said Joe. Joe was feeling pleased with himself because he had just won on Donella and beaten a good horse called Royal Perogative. The sad thing is when Joe Mercer tried to get Boldboy into the starting stalls that day Boldboy threw him off three times. He did not get him into the stalls that day and the race was run without him.

The Major planned to run Boldboy in the Middle Part at Newmarket, a race for top two year olds with classic potential towards the end of the flat racing season, but he had to pass a starting stalls test on the morning of the race. Brian Proctor was given the job of riding Boldboy and getting him to go into the starting stalls. Brian Proctor was employed by the Major full time and rode on the flat for him. He was a very good horseman and jockey and got on well with Boldboy.

When it came to the race at Newmarket Boldboy passed his stalls test all right, Brian Proctor had done a lot of work on him before the stalls test to make sure that he was not too excitable and would not play around. Boldboy went into the stalls OK and Brian Proctor jumped him out in front and they led the field until the last half a furlong. The jockey just pushed Boldboy out with his hands and finished third, beaten by a length.

I asked Brian why he did not give Boldboy a back hander with his whip. He said Lady Beaverbrook had told him that if the horse behaved well he was not to use the whip. 'Well', I said to Brian, 'if you had won you might have been riding the ante post favourite for next year's Two Thousand Guineas'.

One day after the Newmarket race a lad went into Boldboy's box by mistake, and he flew at the lad, broke his head collar and chased the lad out of his box and nearly caught him with his teeth on his back. The lad just managed to get into the feed room and close the door. Another lad called out to me to come and catch the horse before he broke the feed room door down. I got a head collar with a long lead rein on it, went round the corner and there was Boldboy rearing up and striking the feed room door with his two front feet. I spoke in a quiet voice and he turned to me. I gave him a polo mint, put a head collar on him and led him back into his box.

The Major asked Mr Charles Franks the vet to check Boldboy's testicles as I had said it looked as if he only had one. The vet came to look and of course Boldboy put his ears back as soon as he stepped into the doorway of his box. Charles Franks asked me to put my hand up between Boldboy's hind legs and feel if there was a small ball of a testicle above the big one. Boldboy let me touch him and I carefully felt all around his one large testicle but I could not feel anything else.

'It looks like he is a rig or maybe his other testicle has not come down yet and is stuck up in the channel which would account for a lot of his behaviour problems,' said the vet. The next day the Major told me it had been decided to send Boldboy to the Equine Research Centre at Newmarket and that they would put him to sleep with anaesthetic and operate on him. I asked the Major if it meant he would be gelded. The Major said it might well be and he knew how disappointed we would all be after all the hard work we had done with him. Even if he couldn't run in the classic races it would probably be the making of him. Boldboy went to the research centre and after a month he came back to us looking nothing like the horse he was when he went away. He had lost his lovely arched neck, the gloss had gone out of his coat and skin, his hair was long and dull. I was shocked to see him like that. The Major said there was a problem with his other testicle which had not developed properly so he ended up a gelding. It was the right thing to have done with him because he must have had some kind of mental frustration.

However Boldboy enjoyed doing his work on the Gallops and was a changed horse; he was looking good again. One work day Reg Cartwright rode him and Joe Mercer rode a nice horse called Hard Steel. The Major told Reg to lead Joe a good pace until the two furlong mark, before pulling up to go six furlongs. When he had gone four furlongs he was to let Joe come up and let the horses go on and enjoy themselves for the last two furlongs. Boldboy quickened away from Hard Steel and left him a long way behind. The Major was furious and started to tell Reg off as we walked back down the side of the Gallops. 'You went too fast early on and did not give Joe a chance to go with you,' said the Major. Joe Mercer spoke up for Reg and said, 'No, Major, I had every chance to go with them if this horse could but Boldboy is too good for this horse!' The Major never said another word all the way back to the yard; he was deep in thought. I happened to be on one of the next two horses to follow them up the Gallops and it did look as if Boldboy had bolted with Reg or he had gone too fast. Boldboy went to Newbury and ran in the Greenham Stakes which is a race that horses run in as a prep race for the 2,000 Guineas classic. Boldboy won the race very easily at 20-1. Hard Steel went over to Ireland and won the Irish 2,000 Guineas. Boldboy went on to win lots of top class races and became a record holder for winning the most prize money by a gelding on the flat.

The Good and Bad About Parlet

Partlet was a three year old colt who had won a race on the flat. He came from Mr Arthur Bugget's yard. When Partlet arrived at the stable yard we were told that at no time was he to be left without his special muzzle on because he would bite you if he had the chance. The muzzle had two metal bars put across the bottom where the leather had been removed so that he could eat with it on. Also it was policy to have two lads go into his box to tie him up.

Tony Perkins was the lad who looked after Partlet - a very good lad and a great friend of mine. Partlet was what I would call a tall, leggy horse with a good dark colour. He seemed to be happy in the yard and Tony was pleased with him and said he didn't know what all the fuss had been about this horse, he was all right. He did play around in his stable so we put a large ball in his box for him to play with and he had his muzzle left off.

One Sunday Tony Perkins had his Sunday off and I was put down on the list to do Partlet that evening. As with most Sunday evenings the lads that were working would be rushing to get evening stables done on time. As Partlet had been so good and shown no sign of biting anyone I picked his head collar off the hook outside his box and went in to tie him up. When I went into his box and walked towards him he flew at me with his ears flat back and his mouth wide open. He caught hold of my jumper in his teeth and started to rear up, pulling me up by my jumper. I swung the head collar I had in my hand at him and as luck would have it there was a chain on it which had been put on the head collar because he would chew through the rope that was normally used. The chain caught Partlet right across his chest; he let go of me and ran up into the corner of his box and stood shaking. I put his head collar on and carried on as if nothing had happened. Partlet never gave me any trouble after that. He reminded me of a bully I knew at school who did not like it when he got hurt.

The Major took Partlet and three horses over to Mr Guy Knight's place at Lockinge. Guy Knight had a closed in school for schooling horses over small jumps. When we arrived at Lockinge, John Lawrence (Lord Oaksey), the top amateur jockey, was there waiting for us. Tony took Partlet down to the school with another lad on a good old horse who was going to lead Partlet over the small jumps. The Major and John followed. I came with the other lad on the two other horses and we were told to just wait outside.

Of course I wanted to see what was happening in the school so I stood up in my stirrups and could just see inside. The Major legged John up onto Partlet but before he could tell anyone what he would like them to do Partlet went crazy. He roared like a lion, got down on his knees with his eyes rolling in his head, foaming at the mouth and started to bite at the ground, pulling great big pieces of grass turf. The Major shouted to John to get off him and told Tony to take the horse out of the school, put him into the horsebox and take him back to the yard. He was to ask the box driver to come straight back to pick up the other horses.

A few days later the Major sent Partlet and a horse named Felhound, who was a top class hurdler, up to the schooling ground at the top of Simcome Hill. Tony Perkins rode Partlet up to the schooling ground. I was taken up in the Major's Landrover. As soon as Tony came through the gate off the ridgeway onto the schooling ground the Major told me to get onto Partlet

80

and to follow the grey horse, Felhound, over the three hurdles. I wasn't to stop and show Partlet a hurdle first like we normally did, just follow Felhound.

The Major turned to Tim Bate who was riding Felhound and said, 'Don't you stop, just canter down and keep on cantering as you turn and face the three hurdles. Don't stop whatever might happen with Partlet.' Tony got off Partlet and gave me a leg up; he told me to get a good hold of the horse and keep him on the bridle and give him a slap if he dropped his bit. As soon as I was up and in the saddle I got a good hold of the reins and turned in the direction of Felhound who stood about ten lengths away from Partlet. This was because Partlet would try and bite other horses. I gave Partlet a quick sharp slap down his shoulder and took off after Felhound. As soon as Tim saw me set off he started down to the other end of the schooling ground too.

Partlet was well on the bit and pulling nicely; he was a brilliant mover and flowed over the ground. I am sure he remembered who I was because I had never ridden him before. I was catching Tim Bate up on Felhound so I shouted to him to go on a bit faster and that I was all right. Tim had a quick look round at me and went on faster. As we went round the bend I saw the three full size hurdles. I was a little surprised at this because we would normally school a horse first time over the smaller hurdles. Felhound was a strong horse and knew his hurdling well and as soon as he faced the hurdles he took off with Tim and left me and Partlet six lengths behind them but Partlet was not going to be left and followed him with his ears pricked. I was pleased to see that Tim had kept Felhound to one side of the hurdle and not right in the middle. Felhound jumped well as he went over the first hurdle. When Partlet saw him jump he really took hold of his bit; he looked at the first hurdle and his ears twitched back and forward then he set himself right for the take off and jumped it nicely. Felhound kept going straight on towards the next hurdle and jumped it well. Partlet and I jumped the next hurdle better than the first and we were catching Felhound up. When we came to the third and last hurdle we were just over a length behind. I really asked Partlet to stand off the hurdle and jump; he took off behind Felhound and landed a clear length in front of him. Felhound had made a good jump too so I was delighted with Partlet, he really enjoyed his hurdling. I took some time to pull up and when I did the Gallop man came running up to us and said, 'What is the name of that horse?' I just told him to keep away or the horse might bite him. The Gallop man went on to say he had never seen a young horse jump hurdles so brilliantly before.

I hacked to the Major who looked up at me with his pipe in his mouth and a smile in his eyes and said, 'You can stay on him and take him back to the yard with Felhound. He'll not jump again until he runs.' I was hoping to have a ride on Partlet in a race as I had a professional national hunt jockey's licence and the Major had given me some rides in races already, but the owner, Mr Michael Bailey, was an amateur jockey and of course he wanted to ride Partlet himself. His first race over hurdles was at Sandown Park and the owner rode him but the Major got special permission to let Tony Perkins go down to the start and lead Partlet round.

Mr Michael Bailey rode Partlet quite well and had him placed towards the rear in the race. He started to move into a good position as they all came round the last bend past the pond fence, and began to go past horses. When they came to the last hurdle, there was only one horse in front of Partlet; unfortunately it was one of the best hurdles and jump jockey of the time. The horse was Beaver II and the jockey was Fred Winter. Beaver II and Partlet were neck and neck, right up to the winning post. Beaver II won by a short head, and Partlet was second at 33-1. I did hear Fred Winter say that if he had lost the race, he would have put in an objection because Partlet was trying to bite his horse all the way up to the winning post.

Partlet won the next race he ran in. The next time he ran I was asked to take him to Wincanton because Tony Perkins was not well. I was pleased to be asked. The Major got permission for me to go down to the start in the starter's Landrover. As soon as I led Partlet onto the racecourse, Mr Michael Bailey said, 'OK, I'll be alright now'. I let go of Partlet and let the lead rein slide from his bridle, and ran across to the middle of the course where the starter's Landrover was parked and jumped into it. As the starter drove I looked out of the window and watched Partlet cantering down to the start. He had his ears pricked up and was going at a nice pace, not too fast. The evening before I had gone to see how Tony Perkins was and we talked about Partlet and the race. Tony told me to keep Partlet well away from the other runners down at the start and to make sure that when I led him up to the gate tape, for the start of the race, to put him right up by running rail, on his off side so Michael Bailey could turn Partlet's head that way and there would not be any horses there for him to bite.

When I put the lead rein on to Partlet at the start I looked up at Michael Bailey; he was looking tense. To relax him, I said jokingly that I would have the best ride back in the starter's Landrover and I didn't think the starter would try and bite me. Michael gave a little smile.

'Anyway, if you get away well let Partlet run along in front; as soon as he jumps the first hurdle he will be looking for the next hurdle to jump'. I led Partlet right up close to the far rail. When the starter called them to line up to the tape Partlet got off well at the start and was in front when he jumped the first hurdle. He led all the way and won easily. I had got back into the starter's Landrover to come back to the paddock enclosure.

The starter and I watched the horses running down the far side of the course. The starter said, 'I think your horse is not going to bite. He's making all the running and is well clear of the other runners. It looks like he's running away with his jockey. 'Oh no, he's not,' I said, 'The horse has a long stride, and he's cruising along, he takes one stride to most horses' two strides. Just you look how we will go at the hurdles.' When Partlet went past the winning post he had won the race easily. The starter patted me on the back and said, 'You were right, well done.'

Partlet had won three hurdle races in a row. The day he was going to have his fourth race we had a horsebox driver who had never taken Partlet to the races before. The driver parked the horsebox at the side of the lawn. He dropped the ramp down on to the lawn, and then moved all the partitions so that Partlet would have plenty of room. Partlet always travelled to the race on his own in the horsebox with no other horses with him. The horse box driver started shouting, 'Come on let's get this horse to the races'. I think the driver was showing off because he could see Major Dennistoun walking up the drive to the yard. Tony Perkins loaded up Partlet into the horse box, and tied him up to the ring, behind the driver's seat. Then Tony helped the· driver to close up the ramp. He then said to the driver, 'I'll just get my coat out of the tack room'. The driver shouted 'Well bloody well hurry up' and then got into the driver's seat in the horsebox. As Tony Perkins came out of the tack room there was a great big deep roar, like the sound of a lion, and the horse box shook from side to side. The driver fell out on to the ground with a big tear in his shirt and with a face that looked as if all the blood had drained away and as white as a sheet. The Major had by this time got to where the horsebox was parked and helped the driver up off the ground, and was calming him down.

The driver said he wouldn't be taking Partlet to the races and that the bloody horse was a bloody lunatic and a savage. In the end Major Ginger Dennistoun promised the driver money to buy a new shirt and said that we would unload Partlet and put him in the near side stall so that he was not right behind him. We would muzzle him and tie him with two chains. The driver agreed but was kept out of the sight of Partlet until he was reloaded into the horsebox, then he got in and they drove away down the drive. I asked the Major as we both watched the horsebox go down the road if Partlet would be alright. 'Yes', said the Major, 'If that silly ass of a box driver had not been shouting his head off he would not have gone for him, but maybe Partlet has run enough races.' Partlet did win that day, making it four hurdle races he had now won. Eventually he was gelded when he was five years old. Most of his racing spirit went out of him after that.

I would like to mention Peter Wafford who looked after Partlet when he came to Mr Arthur Bugget's yard. Years later I met Peter Wafford and we rode out together. He spoke about Partlet and he was surprised about me schooling Parlett and listened to everything that had happened with the horse when he was at Major Ginger Dennistoun's. Partlet won a flat race at Newmarket when Peter Wafford looked after him. Peter took Partlet out on his own with no other horse because he would try and bite any horse that came near him. Peter made Partlet manageable. Peter Wafford was a good friend. It was a sad day when I heard he had passed away.

Mr and Mrs Bodem

One day when I went to see Joy Bassett she asked me to go and collect some weed killer for the weeds in her paddocks, from a Mr Henry Magwick who had moved into the bungalow which was next to the paddocks. I went and knocked on the kitchen door. He called out, 'The door is open, come in'. I entered the kitchen and there was Mr Magwick with his hand in a large sink cleaning a water colour painting which was floating in water. I noticed that there were a lot of paint brushes about. I asked him if he was an artist.

'Oh, no, I wish I was. A retired antique dealer is what I am', he replied. He then asked me if I was an artist. I said that I did a little bit of drawing and some oil painting. He said he would like to see some of my pictures and to bring some for him to see.

I forgot about what he had said because I thought he was just being kind until one day he was driving through the village and happened to see me. He stopped his car and called to me from across the other side of the road. 'Alwin, you never brought your art work up for me to have a look at. Could you bring them up tonight at about 7 p.m.?' I said OK and went up to see him with some of my pictures that evening. He introduced me to his wife and carefully laid out the pictures on a large table. He looked at them for quite a while and never said anything. Then the telephone rang, he went to answer it, and when he came back he said that he and his wife had to go out in a hurry to see a friend who had a problem and was sorry that he hadn't time to speak to me. The next day I had a phone call from him asking me to come and see him as he would like to talk to me about my art work. I went over and he said he and his wife were sorry about the other evening but they had been discussing my art work and that they would like to help me. They said that there was an artist who gave art lessons but they thought that he could not teach me anything more. Mr Magwick said that he and his wife would like me to go up to London one Saturday and stay all day working in Mr Leonard Boden's studio doing a life class and they would pay for me to do it. I said I would love to but I would pay for it myself.

It was arranged and I went up to London by train from Didcot station to Paddington early on a Saturday morning, caught a number 27 bus to Kensington High Street and then walked a little way to Warwick Gardens. As I walked down the road I saw a man standing just inside a gate. I was looking up at each house to see what numbers were on the doors when I came to the man at the gate. He smiled at me and said, 'You must be Alwin. I am Leonard Boden. Mr Magwick told me all about you.' We shook hands and he led me down the side of his house to a back yard and into his studio, which reminded me of an old Victorian schoolroom. There was a platform about a foot high with a chair with gold gilt on it, and three electrical heaters placed, one at the front of the platform and one at each side. The platform faced three very large windows which gave a lot of north light, which is the preferred light for painting. The electric heaters where put on for the models to make sure they kept warm. Mr Boden asked me if I would help to put the easels in a semi-circle round the front of the platform. He gave me a board and cartridge paper and pins and said he would like me to do a drawing of the head of the model first.

By 9 o'clock most of the other students had arrived and put up their boards and the lady model sat in the gilt chair. Mr Boden asked the model if she was comfortable and warm enough. I was feeling uneasy and embarrassed to see a young lady sitting in front of me with nothing on. Mr Boden walked round to each student and spoke to them about what they should be doing. When he came to me he said, 'It's no good you hiding behind your board, you won't see anything, you must study and take in all the very small details to get a good likeness of the person you are going to paint or draw.'

Feeling that I must do something with this big white sheet of paper I began to draw and of course, once I started, all other thoughts went out of my head. It seemed like no time at all before I heard Mr Boden say, 'It's time for a ten minute break'. This break was for the model so that she could move about. Every twenty minutes we stopped for ten minutes. At twelve o'clock we had an hour's lunch break, then we worked from one o'clock to five.

Mr Leonard Boden was a portrait painter and had done a lot of portraits of the Royal family, also a portrait of the Pope which I believe hangs in the Vatican in Rome. In the lunch break, I had a look round the walls in the studio. There was a marvellous portrait of Mr Tito Gobbi, the famous opera singer, as Scarpia in the opera Tosca. The portrait was one of two done by Mr Boden. The day at the studio went by very quickly. Next day I took the drawing I had done to show Mr Magwick and we talked about it. I remember saying how pleased I was and it was so good to be able to work in Mr Boden's studio.

At the time I went to Mr Boden's studio, he was working on a portrait of Mrs Margaret Thatcher, the Prime Minister, for the Carlton Club in London. I met some very interesting people. I have a book signed by Mr Boden and Mr Tito Gobbi. The book is Tito Gobbi's own autobiography called 'My Life'.

Brigadier Gerard

Brigadier Gerard was broken in at Mr John Hislop's stud then he came into training with the Major. The first day he was taken out for exercise Jim Foggarty and I took him into the sand ring first. The Major stood just outside by the gate, watching us trotting the horse around on long reins. The Major said, 'he seems a quiet sort of horse, you should be able to ride him now'.

I looked at Jim as he turned to the Major and said, 'Major, you haven't seen anything yet. In a moment to be sure when I tighten his girth up we will know what kind of a quiet horse he would like to be.'

When Jim and I put the saddle on he had put his back up and jumped round the box a bit so we left his girth a bit loose.

'With a good lunge in the sand ring he should be alright,' said Jim, 'then you can ride him'. Brigadier Gerard stood and let Jim tighten up his girth. I had hold of the long reins and was standing in the centre of the sand ring. Jim walked up to me and whispered, 'This horse is going to have a right go. You hold the rein that goes round his quarters and I'll hold the one at his head.' The horse just stood and did not move then he turned his head towards us and looked at us for a moment. When we asked him to move he exploded and jumped into the air with all four legs and kicked. I kept him going forward with the long rein that was behind him. After he had let off his energy going round in the soft sand he knew he was beaten and settled down and trotted round nicely again.

Jim said, 'Would you like to see him ridden in the cover ride now, Major?'

The Major said, 'Do you think he will be alright now?'

'Oh to be sure, Major', said Jim, 'he's only be after having a bit of fun with us'.

We led Brigadier Gerard into the cover ride and the Major shut the two big doors and went up into the owner's observation room to watch us. Jim removed the long reins and legged me up into the saddle. I walked him until we had gone round the first bend then I asked him to trot on. He did think of trying me on but I was too quick and he broke into a hack canter. We went past Jim, who was standing by the big entrance doors, at a very sedate pace, and when we came round the bend the next time I pulled up right by Jim. 'He feels like a real nice horse with a good mouth on him too,' I said. The Major was pleased and said of course he was a good ride, Mr John Hislop had said so.

There were a couple of things about Brigadier Gerard that came to light later on. He was a good ride but one day he whipped round and dumped his lad on the floor then ran towards the back of the string of horses, neighing and trying to get to a pony at the very back which was being ridden by a new apprentice. Luckily he was caught and he never ever got to see the pony again. It was discovered that Brigadier Gerard had been turned out with a small pony when he was weaned from his mother. The thing was he had learnt a new trick of how to get anyone off his back by whipping round, at the same time dropping his shoulder to unbalance the lad on top. One day I was on the list of horses to go through the starting stalls to ride Brigadier Gerard with two other horses, a grey horse called Grey Sky and a bay horse called Hinterland.

When an ex-flat jockey named Danny O'Shea gave me a leg onto Brigadier Gerard he said, 'Watch out for this horse, he is being a right sod lately, be careful or he will dump you too'. Danny was right, somehow Brigadier Gerard had developed some bad habits.

I had not ridden him since he first came into the yard but I am sure as soon as I spoke he knew who I was. As we went up to the Winter Gallops Danny O'Shea rode behind me so that he could see what happened when we did our first canter. Having heard about Brigadier Gerard whipping round at the start of a canter I was prepared for what he might do and sure enough he tried it on with me but as he came round and dropped his shoulder he swung right into my whip. Not that I was going to hit him with it, but it gave him a shock and he really took hold of his bit. When it came to putting him through the starting stalls he was good. The Major told us to walk the horses through once, then we had to stand for a while in the stalls.

The horses were all doing well so the Major said he would like us to jump them out and let them run for two furlongs and then pull up. Mr Bobby Elliot was on the grey horse; I can't remember who was riding the bay Hinterland. All three horses went into the stalls OK and when the Major said 'Go,' the stalls sprang open and Brigadier Gerard and I shot out and didn't even see the other two horses. I pulled up and looked back; the grey horse was a long way behind. I asked Bobby Elliot what had happened, did he not jump out of the stalls. 'Yes, we jumped out of the starting stalls alright, but we just could not go with that horse.'

I must say this about riding a horse with a whip. When I first went into racing the head lad said to me, 'Don't forget to ride out with your balancing pole.'

'What's that?' I asked.

'Your whip,' said the head lad, 'and don't let me ever see you hit a horse unless you have to, and then you should only have to hit once and make sure you hit it properly. One good crack is all you should need'.

'But I'm only riding that little filly and she is a Christian of a ride', I said.

'Yes, she is, but it is not the filly. What would you do if a big colt took a fancy to that filly and tried to mount her? Without a whip you would not be able to stop him'.

I always carried a whip but not when riding the yearlings. The Major did not let the lads ride yearlings out with whips, not until they had turned two year olds. He would not tolerate anyone hurting a horse because it could easily be ruined by a bad tempered lad.

I can remember a time when a new lad started work on the Monday morning. He was riding a horse out and had not gone a mile along the road when it started playing up a bit. The Major went alongside this lad on his hack and started shouting at him. 'Ride, you couldn't ride my wife's bike. You are sat on that horse like a sack of s--t. You told me you could ride anything. You couldn't even sit straight in bed'. The Major turned and shouted to the head lad, 'Take this miserable specimen of a lad back to the yard, I don't want to see him again'. When we came back in from exercise the lad was gone, never to be seen again.

It is history now but Brigadier Gerard went to Newbury for his first race and won easily. He was only beaten once, and the day he was beaten I was at York races. After the race I was walking across the middle of York racecourse when I met Mr John Hislop all on his own. I said I was sorry to see a great horse beaten. As I looked up at Mr Hislop there were tears running down his face. To cheer him up I said, 'It took a Derby winner to beat him and I hear they broke the course record'.

I don't know what you think about superstition but this is a story about the lad that looked after Brigadier Gerard, Larry William. He was given Brigadier Gerard to do at evening stables as an extra spare horse to do the day I first rode Brigadier Gerard in the cover ride. Larry Williams came to me to ask me to help catch him in his box because he was going round a bit. I caught him and tied him up for Larry but the horse would still not settle as he was the last horse to go out for exercise that morning. When the Major came round to do evening inspection he had with him the ex-trainer, Mr R.J. Colling. According to what Larry Williams told me, Mr R.J. Colling said of all the yearlings he had seen this horse was the one he would pick because of his build and scope and the way he stood and had a look about him. I told Larry Williams he'd better ask the head lad if he could do him before someone else did so Larry was given Brigadier Gerard to do. Of course he did a really good job of it, but the Major never ever let Larry sit on Brigadier Gerard's back, not even to have his photo taken. When Brigadier Gerard won his first race at Newbury Larry Williams, who was superstitious, kept all of the clothes he had worn, even right down to his socks and shoes, and only wore them when he took Brigadier Gerard to the races. However, the day Brigadier Gerard got beaten at York it was a very hot day so when he led him round the parade ring he left off his sports jacket. Larry told me he thought he had broken his luck by leaving his sports jacket off. I said it was a good job he hadn't left off anything else or he would not have finished the first three!

Brigadier Gerard developed a habit of weaving his head from side to side in front of the painted walls in his box. He would put his head so close to the wall that he would just brush the hair on his face by the white spot mark. By doing this it turned the hair there dark and this can be seen in the photos taken of his head. It was not a problem to him; he still went on winning races.

Bob Turner was a travelling head lad for the Major and after Brigadier Gerard had won his first race at Newbury he became his permanent exercise lad. They got on well and they stayed together all the time until Brigadier Gerard went to stud. Bob Turner is a great friend of mine and we would talk about Brigadier Gerard a lot. Bob said that once the horse had got to know him he was the best ride he could have wished for. Bob used to always ask me when was Brigadier Gerard's next race. 'Why?' I would ask.

Bob would have a little smile on his face and say, 'You know this horse is so turned off and laid back, it is so easy for him to do his work that I have to wake him up just before he runs.' Bob did a wonderful job with Brigadier Gerard and as the saying goes, good lads make good horses and good horses make good jockeys.

Mr Ian Balding, trainer of "Mill Reef"

In 2010 Mr. Ian Balding very kindly invited a group of retired injured jockey's from "Oaksey House", Lambourn, to have a morning at Kingsclere stables.

When we all arrived everyone was made welcome and given coffee and bacon sandwiches. After the coffee we all walked up to the gallops near the stables yard to watch the horses work. As I stood watching the horses do their work it reminded me of Major Hern and the symmetrical way he would do it - horses going up the gallop, with a few lengths between each one in a very well ordered fashion. Then after seeing the horses do their work we all walked back towards the stable yard with me walking a little way behind the group because my left knee was hurting a bit. I damaged my knee years ago when a horse fell down on it. Lucky it was not too bad at the time, but as one gets older, these things start to hurt again.

Ian had taken Lord Oaksey in his Jeep to see the horses on the gallops. On the way back to the stable yard, Ian stopped his jeep and called out to me, saying "Come on. Alwin, get in the jeep with us: So into the jeep I climbed with just Lord Oaksey, Ian and myself. We arrived back at the stables and Ian said he would take us up to the gallops on top of the downs. As he drove his jeep through the stable yard he stopped right beside a very pretty girl, bent over tightening up her saddle and bridle, ready to peck up her bottom, which was stuck right up in the air. And it was a very neat bottom with her tight jodhpur bitches making it look even more as if she really had nothing on under her britches. Ian asked her how her horse was. The girl turned her head with a cheeky smile on her face and answered, 'He is very well sir.'

'Good,' answered Ian, then drove off - slowly. Looking at me in the mirror he said, "Well Alwin, how would you like to be following that pretty backside up the gallops?'

'Ho,' I said, 'if I was watching that all the morning, I would be going cross-eyed.' Lord Oaksey and Ian burst out laughing. A wonderful sense of humour is what most jockeys have. It helps you to forget the bad times.

We arrived at the top of the downs. Ian stopped the jeep right by the place he would stand and watch the horses come up the gallop going by him. He started to tell Lord Oaksey and I of the terrible day when the marvellous horse, Mill Reef, came up the gallop working so well. And just as he past Ian he changed his legs unexpectedly and was pulled up. Mill Reef stood holding his near leg off the ground.

Ian carried on telling us, with emotion in his voice, how they brought a horsebox up onto the gallops and stopped as near as they could to Mill Reef who had not moved. Ian, trainer of Mill Reef, dropped the horsebox ramp right in front of the horse. When they said to him, "come on", he walked on three legs and sprang into the horsebox, landing on his good front legs without the broken one touching the floor. When he arrived back at the stable yard he was unloaded from the horsebox, which was parked as near as possible to the big room that had been made ready for him. He walked down the horsebox ramp, on just three legs, without the broken leg touching the ground. He stood with large bales of straw stacked round him, with a sling put around his stomach, which hung from the ceiling and made sure he did not fall onto the floor.

Mill Reef was a very sensible horse. He never panicked. A vet examined his leg, and said he would have to put it in plaster. Then it all depended on how Mill Reef would react on coming round from the anaesthetic. When it wore off the vet went on to say that there had been a very good filly racehorse in America who had a very similar break in the leg. But when she came round after the operation she went crazy and killed herself. But when Mill Reef came round, he was relaxed and calm. He was a very good patient and his leg healed well. Mr. Balding did say that after Mill Reef went to stand at stud his temperament changed and he became a bit savage.

Mill Reef died when he was fifteen years old.

Injured Jockey's from Oaksey House at Ian Balding's Yard 2010 in front of statue to Mill Reef

Joy Bassett and Lady Freak's dogs

One summer's evening I was lunging a young horse round in Joy Bassett's paddock. After a while she came out with Lady Freak and they stood and watched me. Lady Freak had a loud voice and sounded more like a man when she spoke. Joy Bassett was not very melodious either. When they first came and leant on the paddock rails they were laughing and joking with each other. Joy Bassett had brought her dogs, all of them; Lady Freak had her dogs too. Suddenly there was a loud yelp from one of Lady Freak's dogs. We all looked towards where the sound had come from and there was one dog being covered by one of Joy Bassett's dogs; they were locked together. The language that came from Lady Freak's mouth was so bad I can't write it down. She screamed at Miss Joy Bassett to do something to get that f------ dog of hers off her beautiful breed dog.

Joy Bassett shouted back, 'You stupid old cow, why did you bring your dog out if she is in season?'

I stood and watched as the pantomime got worse.

'Well don't stand there,' shouted Lady Freak to Miss Bassett, 'we must get a big tub of water and throw it over them to get them apart!'

So off they went, still shouting at each other and calling each other names. A few minutes later they came back carrying a small bath of cold water, Lady Freak holding the handle on one side and Miss Bassett the other. They were still shouting at each other.

With all the shouting going on all the dogs began to bark and were running round the two dogs locked together. Just as they swung back to pour it over the two dogs Lady Freak was tipped up by one of her other dogs and she fell down and brought down Miss Bassett too.

The water went up into the air and came down over the two women and the two dogs. It had the desired effect on the two dogs, they parted, but by this time nearly every dog in the village had come into the paddock barking and chasing Lady Freak's bitch.

I can still see Lady Freak with her hat in one hand and water dripping out of her dress, running after her dogs. Miss Joy Bassett just sat on the ground laughing.

Sad Joke

Mr Charlie Spares was an ex-flat jockey who had won the Epsom Derby on a horse called Arctic Prince. He worked for the Major and was a real character. He loved to play jokes on the other lads in the yard. He would take a lad's grooming kit and put it on top of the muck hill. Sometimes he would creep up to a box and see if there was anyone inside with a horse. If there was anyone there he would shut the top door up, bolt it and switch off the light then run off laughing.

One day he went too far with his jokes. Normally at evening stable time we would take out the horses' water buckets and stand them outside the stable while we carried on mucking out. Charlie Spares got a long lunging rein and tied up about three buckets which stood outside three different boxes and hid round the corner. He pulled on the lunging rein and all the water buckets went over making a hell of a noise; the horses in the stables jumped around with the shock of the clatter. The lads came out of the stables to see what was going on and Charlie could not stop himself from laughing, he was doubled up. The three lads that had been in the stables ran after him and caught him. They carried him down to the paddock rails near the drive, stripped him absolutely naked and tied him up to the railings with the lunge rein he had used on the buckets. Charlie was screaming like mad. To top it all they got hold of a large bunch of stinging nettles and stuck them right up between his legs and then they left him there. He kept shouting for someone to come and untie him but to add to poor Charlie's humiliation, the lady secretary and housekeeper came along the drive. They stopped and looked and burst out laughing at him then quickly went on their way. I must say it was a funny thing to see - this little, round, naked body with a bunch of stinging nettles sticking out of his bum.

When the ladies had gone I went with another lad and untied him. He was swearing and crying. 'Take these bloody nettles away!' His bottom was covered in little white lumps made by the nettles. It looked very painful and he could hardly walk or sit down and was off work a few days. We all got a right bollocking from the Major who said that we could have killed Charlie and if it happened to a horse he would have had a vet to give it an injection.

Many years later I had reason to remember the Major's words. I was riding a yearling in the paddock with two other yearlings. One of the lads that was riding with me told me to watch out for the one I was riding because the day before he had rubbed up against a hedge then gone down onto the ground and got rid of the lad that was riding him and ran loose. All the time I was riding this yearling I had a feeling he was waiting for a chance to do something. The other two lads said he would be all right and to keep in between them, and so he was for a long time. Just as we were going to take them in, the yearling I was on went down. I stepped off him and sat on his head so that he could not get up. He was flat on his side with his legs stuck out trying to kick and get up. I kept him there on the ground for a few minutes then I got off and let him up. He was shaking and I noticed he had laid down in a patch of stinging nettles. I took him straight into his box and ran to the office to telephone for a vet. The vet was very quick in coming and gave the yearling an injection. He got over it alright and he did not forget it either.

A year later this same horse had a little bump on his back and had to be lunged in the sand ring for a couple of days, then a small lad was put down to ride him out. The horse took umbrage at this and would stop when in the cover ride and jumped and kicked which made a lot of trouble with all the other horses. The Major said to me we would stop his little game and give him something else to think of.

'You, Alwin, and I, will take him up to the schooling ground and put him over some hurdles'. I had not ridden the horse since he was a yearling but I am sure he had not forgotten the stinging nettles. He gave me a great ride over the hurdles and I rode him out nearly every day. He then ran in a race at Kempton and won first time on a racecourse.

A Joke That Was Not Nice

I really don't know if I should write this; it was the worst joke I have ever heard of, and knowing the two people involved makes it all the more funny.

A young couple were going to get married. The lad was very quiet and he thought the world of his fiancée. We asked him where he was taking his wife for their honeymoon. 'I don't know, I would like it to be a nice surprise for her, but I can't afford much', answered the lad.

An older lad said, 'I might be able to help you out. I have a small caravan at the seaside; you can have it for two weeks for nothing as a wedding present'.

'Thanks very much!' said the lad. 'Are you sure you don't mind?'

'You'd better make sure your fiancée agrees to it, because it is only a small caravan,' said the older lad.

'I'll ask her tonight,' said the lad.

As he went off to tell his fiancée, the older lad began to laugh. I asked what he was laughing about. He said, 'You'll know if it all goes to plan'. Then he asked me what I thought of the lady that the lad was going to marry. I told him that she was a very nice person and she went to church on Sunday.

'Yes, I know that,' said the older lad, 'but I think she is a bit snooty. Do you thing they have been to bed together?'

'No,' I said, 'her mother and father keep a close watch on her and are very strict'.

The wedding took place over forty years ago and the caravan did not have all the modern conveniences that caravans have today. The lad that was getting married asked if he could go and see the caravan before the wedding. The older lad said he would take him on Sunday. On Monday, I asked the lad who was getting married if the caravan was alright for him and his fiancée. 'It's a bit small, but it's in a nice spot and I am sure my fiancée will find it very romantic'.

'What do you do about going to the toilet; has it got a toilet inside the caravan?' I asked.

'No! But there is a toilet and a shower room on the caravan site and if we have to go in the night there is a large china pot to use'.

It was a nice wedding; we did their car up with ribbons, and put a 'just married' sign on the back and tin cans tied on with string that dragged along the road when they set off for their honeymoon.

When they came back from their honeymoon the young lad could not wait to get at the lad that had let him have the use of his caravan. He hit him and started fighting him. When we separated them, we managed to find out what had made the young lad so angry.

What had happened was this. When they got to the caravan at the seaside it was very late, so they went straight to bed and they consummated the marriage. Afterwards the lady had to go to the toilet on the china pot. She screamed, 'What have you been and done to me?' at her husband. He put on the lights to see what she was screaming about. There she was crying her eyes out sitting on the china pot with all this foaming white and pink bubbles coming out round her naked feet.

The older lad had gone to the caravan the day before the wedding and had put two tins of Andrews Liver Salts into the china pot. As soon as the lady used it, it was as if it had water added which made it froth up and sparkle with bubbles.

The young lad never forgave the older lad and he told me that his wife thought that he himself had done it for a joke on her. I can say it did not spoil the marriage; they had three children and are still married.

John Francome's Luck

'Born Lucky', the book written by Mr John Francome, the champion National Hunt jockey, was given to me by Mr and Mrs Tom Marks as a Christmas present. I did enjoy reading it; it brought back a lot of memories for me. Kindly John Francome had written in the book, 'Good Luck to Alwin's Boy and Soumark' and signed it.

When I first met Mr and Mrs Marks they were looking to buy a racehorse for National Hunt racing. As it happened Miss Joy Bassett had a big leggy two year old for sale which I had handled since it was born. I thought a lot of this horse and Mr and Mrs Marks agreed to buy him, they also bought a yearling filly. The filly was named Soumark and the big two year old was named after me, Alwin's Boy. It was very nice of Mr and Mrs Marks to name their horse like that. Some lads would call me, 'Alwin or be second'. To tell about all the bad luck these two horses had would take too long. Both were sent to Newmarket to be trained. Soumark's first race was when she was a three year old and it was on the flat at Wolverhampton. As could be seen on the video recording she might well have won had she come out of the stalls alright, but she came out twenty lengths behind and finished fourth, not far off the winner. Her jockey said if they had got out of the stalls with the other runners they might have won.

Mr and Mrs Marks moved the two horses back from Newmarket, but when they came back they developed leg problems. Mr Charles Frank looked at Alwin's Boy's leg and then said the best thing to do with him was to give him a complete rest, bring him back in six months, hack him around and, to help get him fit, take him cub hunting. When Alwin's Boy did run in a novice hurdle at Towcester, jockey Hewel Davis rode.

Hewel Davis was first jockey for Captain Tim Forster and rode Alwin's Boy. When I went through the entrance into the racecourse paddock to my surprise Bob Turner and his wife Monica were waiting for me. They had not said they would be coming. Bob smiled and said, 'We only came because you said this horse is really good and if you said it is a good horse it must be'.

Alwin's Boy ran a wonderful race, he was flying at the end and finished not beaten far in third place at 33-1. Hewel Davis said what a lovely horse he was and could not stop talking about him. But after such a promising start to his racing career Alwin's Boy had a lot of things go wrong. He was second twice, but he really wasn't right within himself.

Mr Charles Frank, the vet, looked at Soumark and the slight leg injury she had and said to do the same with her as with Alwin's Boy - rest her. She was not very old so the best thing would be to put her in foal, and that would make sure her leg would have a good rest. So Soumark was put in foal and had a nice foal. When she was being prepared to go back into training it was very plain she had her mind on other things. She was put in foal again and had duly delivered, but this time when we started to ride her she was in the right frame of mind. However, she had a little setback in training and did not look like winning a race. You need a bit of luck sometimes. Her bad luck was when she really looked well at Stratford a young jockey was riding her. Soumark was going well when she made a big jump and the jockey was unseated.

If you believe in people passing on their good luck I can tell you, after Mr John Francome signed his book and wrote 'Good Luck to Alwin's Boy and Soumark they both won.

Alwin's Boy won at Ludlow, price 12-1, and Soumark also won at Ludlow, price 50-1. It was one of those great days you have in racing. The day Soumark won at Ludlow I was walking into the weighing room when I met Johnny Buckingham, the ex-jockey who had ridden Foinavon to win the Grand National at 100-1. Johnny Buckingham was a great friend. He asked me what I was doing there and I told him I had an interest in a mare that was running, in fact this mare reminded me of a mare that he had ridden a lot of winners on, called Neapolitan Lou. If she was anything as good as her she must have a chance.

I said to him, 'If Soumark doesn't win today I don't think she will ever win'.

When I went into the winners' enclosure Johnny Buckingham shook my hand and said, 'Well done, you are so right, she is a bit like Neapolitan Lou.'

Dave Dick Walk

One day, coming home from Ludlow races, the Major gave a lift to David Dick, the National Jockey. He was a very tall man for a jockey. He won the Grand National at Aintree on a horse called E.S.B.

David Dick sat in the back of the car beside me, right behind the Major who was in the front seat but he was not driving; his wife, Nancy, was driving the car. We had been travelling for about half an hour when the Major lit up his pipe and it was not long before the car was full of smoke.

David asked the Major to put out his pipe but he said nothing and just kept on puffing away. David asked if he could open the car window a little bit, the Major still said nothing. David turned to me with a big grin on his face and put one finger to his lips then he slipped his long arm to the window handle and very quickly opened the window right down, grabbed hold of the Major by the back of the neck and put his head right through the open window. He then wound up the window so the Major was stuck with his head outside of the car. The Major was screaming like mad. His wife just kept driving along as if nothing was happening.

After a few minutes David opened the window and pulled the Major's head back into the car. His face was blue with cold but he still had his pipe in his mouth. He did not look happy. David jumped right back into his seat and said, 'it was only a joke, Major'.

'Bloody joke was it?' shouted the Major, still trying to get his breath back, 'Not a very clever one. Remember, he who laughs last laughs longer.'

The rest of the journey was very quiet. It is a long drive from Ludlow back to Letcombe Regis and about an hour and a half after the window incident the Major turned to Nancy and said, 'Stop, this is where David lives'. Nancy was going to say something to the Major but he just looked at her so she said nothing. 'Come on, David, move, we haven't got all night', said the Major.

As David was getting out of the car he turned and asked, 'Do I still get the ride on that horse next week?'

'Of course you do, I'll telephone you,' said the Major.

'Thanks,' said David, and closed the car door.

As Nancy drove the car slowly away David was running after us, banging on the side of the car shouting 'stop'. Laughing the Major told Nancy to keep going. Nancy asked how far David had to walk to get home and would he be alright. 'Of course he will', laughed the Major, 'he's a big boy now'.

Embarrassing

As I think of that incident it reminds me of the day I rode a horse called Fellhound at Cheltenham but not at the big Cheltenham Festival meeting.

Fellhound was a very hard horse to ride. Harry Sprague, a top hurdle jockey who had ridden winners on Fellhound, had said that to ride Fellhound was harder than doing a day's hard labour, as Lord Oaksey (John Lawrence) found out, also the flat jockey Jock Wilson in a flat race at Worcester. Fellhound took off with Jock Wilson on the way to the start and went twice round before he could stop him and he had to be withdrawn from the race. I must say that Fellhound was hard to ride but I did get on with him quite well.

Coming down the hill at Cheltenham we were at the front disputing the lead going into the second last when Fellhound dived at the hurdle, met it all wrong and we did well to keep up off the ground. We finished a respectable seventh.

Going home after the race in the Major's car, the owner of Fellhound, Mr Ben Smith, and the Major's daughter, who was about the same age as me were in the back of the car. Ben Smith and the Major were pleased with the way Fellhound had run as it was his first race for a long time. I sat in between Ben Smith and the Major's daughter, Ginny, and went to sleep as I was so tired. When I woke up I had my head right between Ginny's breasts and my arms around her waist. It was one of the most embarrassing moments in my life. I could not stop saying how sorry I was. Ginny and Ben were smiling at me. Ben said, 'You have definitely got the right idea in your dreams'. Ginny didn't say anything, she was a real good sport about it.

Stuck in a Blizzard

The 1962-63 winter was the worst I have ever known. The snow was so deep we had to dig a trench round the stable yard from one stable door to the other. The first day of the snow we mucked out the stables as normal and put the muck on the muck heap.

When the Major came up to the yard the next day he called us all into the tack room and said, 'This bad weather is going to get worse. We must keep the lights on at night to give out some heat and keep the fire going all the time in the tack room. Also we'll have to build a straw ring to get the horses out for exercise.'

He told us to use the old straw from the muck heap to make the straw ring with, and not to muck out the stables but to keep putting lots of new clean straw on top. The heat generating from the muck would help keep the horses warmer.

The Major was right, the weather did get worse. It was so cold. The horses came out for exercise one at a time. The head lad, Don Mills, legged us up and then led us down across what was the path in front of the stables into the paddock. The paddock rails had been removed so we could go straight in onto the straw ring that had been made.

The horses were a bit fresh and excited to be out of their stables at first but they soon felt the cold, even with heavy rugs on and night caps on their heads to keep them warm. After 30 minutes they were glad to get back into the stables. It was so cold at night it froze the water buckets solid in the stables. We had to put them on top of the round stove in the tack room to melt the ice. We all collected whatever blankets we could and old bran sacks to put on the horses to keep them warm.

The bad weather went on week after week, with no horse racing anywhere in the country. After about six weeks a tractor made its way to Wantage and brought back bread and milk to the village.

We had used up nearly all the hay that we had for the horses so the Major asked the farmer who supplied us with hay and straw if he could bring some more. He said he had plenty in his big barn on the down just off of the ridgeway but he could only get there on his big tractor and not with a trailer. He used his tractor to get up to the barn to feed his sheep. The Major asked if he would be able to get to the barn in his Landrover which was a pick up type, 'May be', he said, 'if you keep to the tractor tracks it will not be too bad going up the hill on the main road but when you turn onto the ridgeway make sure you keep to the tractor tracks'.

The next day the Major told Tony Perkins and me to meet him outside his house at 2 p.m. and to make sure we had plenty of clothes on to keep warm. We put a spade and shovel and some sacks in the back of the Landrover and knocked on the Major's door. Out he came, walking like a robot - he had so many clothes on he could hardly bend his knees. His head was covered with a fur hat and he had a scarf tied round his ears.

I said, 'You look as if you are going to the Antarctic.'

He just glared at me and puffed on his pipe.

We all got into the Landrover and off we went, sliding about on the road. We went onto the main road up the hill. The snow was piled up higher than houses on each side and it was only wide enough for one car. We made it to the top of the hill and turned off and started to go along the ridgeway. We could only see the tops of the tall hedges sticking out of the snow. The bark at the top had been eaten away by rabbits and hares which sat there, too weak to move away from the Landrover. It was slow going along the tractor tracks, the snow was scraping on the bottom of the Landrover but we managed to get to the barn. The Major told Tony and me to load up with hay and he would keep the engine going. As we were loading the hay the wind got up and the snow was blowing like a real blizzard. It was stinging my eyes and I could not hold my head up to face it. By the time we had finished loading and tied the hay on, the snow had built up round the wheels. We tried to dig it away but the wind was blowing it back again. The Major tried to drive the Landrover but it was stuck; we put sacks under each wheel but it would not move.

The Major said, 'One of us will have to go and get help and as you're the youngest it will have to be you', he pointed at me. He did look a very sorry sight, he had been sitting in the vehicle with the heater on but the wind was so cold his eyes had gone red with dark rings round them and he was shivering.

I got out of the Landrover and stumbled my way through the snow. The tractor tracks had disappeared; it was one disaster after another. I couldn't go very fast, I fell down in the snow drifts and got covered with snow and it was beginning to get dark. Just when I was really tired I looked up and saw the light of the tractor coming towards me. I waved my arms and the farmer only just managed to see me. He said I looked like a walking snowman. I climbed up onto the back of the tractor and we went to the barn. The Landrover by this time had snow right up to the windows on one side. The tractor pulled it out and towed it all the way back to the main road. The Major did not look very well. I myself ended up with some chilblains and I will always remember Tony Perkins' face with ice hanging from his eyebrows. I am sure if the farmer had not come when he did we would have all died up on the Downs.

It was not one of the Major's lucky years for when the snow started to go he arranged for some of the horses to go to the seaside to gallop along on the sand. Two Lambourn horseboxes came and took the horses to the seaside. It was a long way to travel, and there was still a lot of snow on the side of the roads. When we finally arrived the Major was already there with the trainer F. Walwyn and his horses, which were being unloaded from the horseboxes. The Major rode one of our horses and when we had all been given a leg up he led us down onto the beach and told us that we would gallop back two by two. The horse I was riding was very heavy headed and took a strong hold of the bit in his mouth, and pulled a lot, so after the gallop all the feeling had gone out of my hands and they were numb. Later, travelling back in the horsebox, I had what is called 'hot aches' in my fingers; they were burning with pain and I did not know what to do with them.

The Major was smiling when he looked at each horse after the gallop along the sand, and said, 'Now follow me, we will go into the sea and wash all the sand off the horses' legs'. So off we went following the Major into the sea. The horses seemed to enjoy it but all of a sudden the Major and his horse disappeared into the sea down a hole. The others shot round and ran out of the sea up the beach. I looked back to see what had happened to the Major. He was clinging to his horse's neck, the horse had found his feet and was walking slowly out of the sea with the Major hanging on. The horse stopped just out of the sea and shook himself like a wet dog and the Major fell flat out on the sand while the horse walked slowly away as if nothing had happened. When he could get his breath he was shouting, 'Help! Get me up!' Darky the travelling head lad for F. Walwyn came running down the beach with blankets and one of the horsebox drivers too. They carried the Major back up the beach and put him in a car. The horse he had been riding was OK, nothing wrong with him, only a bit wet. The next day when I went to see the Major I could not help but have a joke with him. I said, 'You did a good job making that horse swim for you yesterday and you didn't mind the cold water. Did the water taste nice or was it salty?'

'It's all right for you stood there taking the p--- out of me', shouted the Major, 'but let it be a lesson to us, we will not be going to the seaside again'.

'Oh, what a shame,' I said, 'I was looking forward to going again for the wonderful entertainment we had!'

Terrorism

I bought a house in a quiet part of a town. When moving in and clearing out the bit and pieces left by the people in the house before me, I found all kinds of things - photos of hooded men stood by a bed, with rows of rockets and ammunition, laid out on the bed, and a map with cross marks on it in red. I knew what it was but I didn't like to say so not knowing what to do, I telephoned John "Lord Oaksey" to ask for advice. Of course he was very helpful. He told me to go to the police station with some of the stuff. And if the police wanted any reference to support my identity he said to give them his name as he was a Justice of the Peace. So I went to the police station, and they were very kind. They could see that I was very worried about it. Straight away they came round to the house, took fingerprints, and took things away with them. The men were all in plain clothes, and well mannered.

A few days later one plain clothes officer knocked on the door, identified himself, and asked if there had been any post from abroad to this address. I told him no. He thanked me for being of help to them. John telephoned a lot during this time to asked how things were going? The police did come again and asked if anyone had called who had lived in the house before. Again I told them no and said that I would let know if anyone should do so. Thankfully I did not hear anymore about it and we soon moved away.

My next meeting with the plain clothes police was when I was going down to Aberdare in Wales, from Bedford travelling at 2 a.m. A car was following me and began to overtake and, after moving alongside, stayed there for sometime before eventually overtaking me and then crossing in front of my car, but with a blue flashing light on the roof. Then one plain clothes officer got out of the car and waved me down. So I stopped and wound down my window. The police officer asked me where I was going at that time of the morning. I gave him my address in Wales. Then he asked what was I doing with the big painting in the back of my car. It was a painting that I had copied, a painting of "Madame Seriziat" by the artist "Jacques-Louis David", which I had seen when I went to Paris and visited the Louvre. Luckily it was written on it that it was a copy and after the officer had a good look he said, 'It's ok. We have checked your car registration and the address you gave us matches. You can carry on.'

The copied painting of "Madame Seriziat" is now in my wife's aunt's house in London.

Madame Seriziat

Still Laughing with John 'Lord Oaksey'

When I was working for Major Dick Hern, the Queen's Trainer, John "Lord Oaksey" came to visit the yard to see the horses and to find something to write about for Horse & Hounds magazine. It was a nice surprise to see John standing by the entrance to the covered ride, watching the horses going round inside.

"How are you Bobby? It's great to see you again. What's the horse you're riding?" he asked.

"Chalton, the Queen's horse," I told him.

"Is he any good Bobby? "

"Yes he is very good and I'm sure he will win the maiden race at Newbury next week. How's your hand shaking going these days John?" I asked in return

He started laughing. "It's good, I've got it to a fine art now. I take hold with one hand to start with and shake the ladies' hand a little bit. Then I hold her hand with both mine. And the ladies like it.!"

I was still laughing with John when Major Hern walked up.

"What is so funny to make you two so happy?

John, still laughing said, "It's a old joke between us."

Chalton did win the maiden race at Newbury and at York. He also ran in the Gold Cup at Royal Ascot. He ran very well.

Zeus

One Saturday morning Major Dennistoun came into the stable where I was saddling up a horse, to ride out for the first lot. 'Nobble,' called out the Major. 'Come down, to my office, after you have ridden that horse.' Knocking on the Major's door I went in thinking that I was going get a bollocking but he smiled at me and said 'you know that John Lawrence has broken his collar bone and cannot ride his horse "Zeus", at Newbury today. He asked me to let you ride out second lot. I will let John Mills know; be back here in one hour ready to go to Newbury with me in my car.'

When I was walking towards the weighing room to get ready to ride. Sir Peter O'Sullivan spoke to me. 'That horse "Zeus" you ride for John Lawrence is a nice horse, you must be pleased to be riding him.'

'Yes, he is a good horse in the race with 37 runners.'

'Good luck,' said Sir Peter.

I came into the weighing room. Robin Lord, my valet, greeted me with Good Morning Professor. I see you are riding his Lordship's horse, and I must make you look your best because your race is on television.

When all jockeys were ready to go out of the weighing room to ride in the race,, Robin Lord stood by the door and said, 'Now you lads remember you are on television so don't used bad language in the paddock. And keep smiling at the camera.'

I could see John standing in the paddock with the Major with his arm in a sling. He gave me a lot of encouragement saying 'You will do well.' The Major was smoking his pipe. He smiled and said, 'Keep out of trouble and let you and the horse enjoy yourselves.'

Zeus felt good under me as we lined up at the start. I

put Zeus up behind Fred Winter and in between David Nicholson -two top jockeys, so I knew their horses would jump well. When the starting tape went up, off we went. Zeus had a good hold of his bit, and jumped the first hurdle well. I kept still on Zeus until we came up the home straight with 13 hurdles to go. I asked Zeus to go fast - he did, going past the other horses. We finished in the first ten. Zeus and I$_t$ really enjoyed the race. The Major and John came to the racecourse to meet us. John was very pleased and excited saying it was wonderful to watch. He jumped so well. He will make a good chaser. The Major looked up at me with a little smile.

'Neither of you got tired then?'

'No, he is a good horse.'

Sadly I never rode him again, but John "Lord Oaksey" did have some good rides on Zeus.

Schooling On My Own

One day I was riding a horse named Monastaire on my own. The Major had told me to take the horse up through the village of Letcombe Regis towards Castle Hill and before I got to the steep bit of the hill I had to turn right through a stubble field and trot the horse round. I was to walk one round, then trot one and continue doing it for an hour, and then return to the yard.

Monastaire had a few quirks and could be a bit wilful. I had seen him whip round and run backwards with some of the lads. Not having ridden him before, I was wondering why I had been put down to ride him out for second lot and being told to just trot round a stubble field was disappointing.

In the stubble field there were rows of straw bales. Having trotted round the field a couple of times and getting to know this horse, I wanted to jump him over the stray bales. Trotting towards the bales, I made him go into a hack canter and jump them. He was not very fluent first time, but he got better as we progressed round the large field.

The horse had taken hold of his bit and was enjoying it. The thrill of sitting on this racehorse and going over jumps was such an exciting feeling. Pleased with myself we went back to the stable yard.

When I was doing the horse up and making him tidy the head lad, Dow Mills, came into the stable and said he would carry on seeing to the horse and I was to go straight down to the Major's office (which was in the house).

'What for?' I asked.

'Don't know,'replied the head lad.

Walking down to the office all sorts of things came into my head but the one thing I had not given any thought to was that he had watched me riding the horse over the straw bales. He had driven up in his Landrover and watched me through his binoculars.

When I got to the Major's office I knocked on the door and he asked me to come in, in a quiet voice. He was sat at his desk looking very serious at me.

'How many times did you jump that horse over the straw bales?'.

'I did not count,' I answered.

'Well I did,' said the Major. 'It was somewhere around twelve times and when I want you to school a horse, I will ask you. Do not do it again without my say so. You can go now.'

Just as I went to the door he suddenly said, 'You can ride the horse schooling with the jockeys on Sunday morning.'

'Thank you very much,' I replied.

When the other lads asked me why I had been summoned to the office, although I was excited, I did not want to tell anyone and I just said, 'nothing worth talking about.'

Inmovable, My First Ride

When I came back to Major Dennistoun, things were very busy and all the stables were full of horses. There was a real buzz about the stable yard. I still lodged with Mr. and Mrs. Palmer. They both loved horse racing. Mrs. Palmer would grumble at me when I did not eat all the lovely food she cooked for me. I would say that I was just going for a run to keep fit and not get fat and heavy. Being so keen, I wanted to be as fit as possible to be a good jockey. I had to keep my weight down.

One day John Lawrence, (now Lord Oaksey), and I were schooling some young horses on the schooling ground with Major Dennistoun looking on as always. The horse John Lawrence was riding started to play up, and the Major started to shout.

"Get hold of that horse and make him go about his work." There was an exchange of words between John and the Major. I did hear John say to the Major, 'Let Bobby ride this one and I'll ride the one he is on.'

"Alright then, get on with it," said the Major as he walked towards the horse I was on to hold it, whilst I jumped off and got onto John's mount. I knew this horse very well. He could be a bit naughty. The horse was a three year old, nice looking, but on the small side.

We cantered down to the start of the three hurdles and let the horses have a really good look at the first hurdle. Then we went to the point which we normally turn in and set off upsides going straight at the first of the three hurdles we would jump. John and I held a nice steady pace and the horses jumped alright for novices. The Major told us to take the horses down again and to do it twice more, letting them go quicker the last time. The horses jumped alright again the second time. My horse was getting on his toes and excited. On the third and last time, I stayed upside of John on his horse over the first two hurdles then John asked his horse to go faster, so I did the same. My horse stood well off the last hurdle and seemed to fly over it. John's horse jumped ok but the horse I was on landed a good length clear of his.

When we pulled up and walked over to the Major, he asked John what he thought.

"You should let Bobby ride that horse when he runs. He will do a good job on him," he said.

The Major did not say anything at the time, but at evening stable when he was looking round all the horses as he did every evening, he looked at me and said, "You can ride that horse you schooled this morning at Kempton next week."

"Thank you very much," I said. The head lad, Don Mills, looked at the Major and said,

"Bobby has not got a licence yet sir."

The Major quickly replied, "All he needs for his first ride in public is a letter from me. After that, all being well, he will have a full jockey's licence." I was so pleased and excited.

On the day of the race the Major had declared two runners in the same race. John Lawrence was to ride one which was a short price in the betting and I was to ride the horse I had schooled. His name was Immovable. When we went in the jockey's changing room John Lawrence introduced me to Robin Lord who was to become my valet too.

I was called Professor or Ollie, but mainly called Bobby.

Robin Lord was my racing valet and when I entered

128

the jockey's changing room he would always greet me by saying, "Good morning Professor, what can I do for you today?" I never did find out why he called me the Professor, but we got on very well and he helped me a lot.

When we both came out into the paddock to ride in the race, we walked together up to the Major and the owners. The best thing any trainer could have said to me at that time, as I stood there thinking I mustn't make any mistakes, came from the Major who said, "Go out there and enjoy yourself Bobby, but don't get in the way of John Lawrence."

The horse Immovable started well. The starting gate went up, and off he went taking a good hold of the bit. After we jumped the first jump we were in front, passing the big stand. I sat as still as I could, the horse Immovable was really going well. We jumped the fourth hurdle and some of the other horses came upside of us so I took a little pull and looked to see if John Lawrence was coming. I could not see him at all. Johnny Gilbert came upside of me and said he didn't think this horse was going to finish the race. He was hard at work on the horse, pushing and kicking. I watched him for a few strides and then I did the same. My horse found another gear and went sailing past some of the other runners coming round the bend into the straight. I was catching up with the leader and when we were coming up to the last hurdle, a horse that was a few lengths in front of me fell. I quickly moved Immovable so he would not land on top of the fallen horse and jockey. We finished in fourth place.

The Major came out onto the racecourse and led me in. Straight away I asked what had happened to John Lawrence. The Major replied that his horse did not jump the first hurdle very well and nearly fell, so he pulled him up. The Major carried on talking to me saying he was pleased to see me use my brain and avoid jumping on top of the horse which had fallen in front of me.

Don Mills, the head lad, took the reins off the Major and carried on leading into the fourth place. With a smile on his face Don said,

"Now you know what it is really like to ride in a race, well done."

That was the start of me having rides for Major John Dennistoun and I will always be thankful to Lord Oaksey for his help. I had a wonderful ride on his horse, Zeus, at Newbury which was a great thrill, finishing in the first ten of thirty-seven runners.

Having had one or two rides for the Major, I was given a ride on Fellhound in a race at Cheltenham but not the Cheltenham Festival Meeting. Fellhound was a very hard horse to ride. Harry Sprague, a top jockey who had ridden winners on Fellhound had said that to ride Fellhound was harder than doing a day's hard labour. Lord Oaksey, and the flat jockey Jock Wilson found this out. Jock Wilson rode Fellhound in a flat race at Worcester. Fellhound took off with him on the way to the start and went twice round the course before he could stop him. He had to be withdrawn from the race. I must say that Fellhound was hard to ride, but I did get on with him quite well.

Ear Operation.

My bad ear began to discharge again and I had to have another operation in the John Radcliffe hospital, Oxford, under Mr. McBeth, who I found out many years later was known as the best ear surgeon!. Another ear and nose specialist who was checking my ear later told me he had worked with Mr. McBeth in the John Radcliffe and he said he had done a wonderful job. But after the operation I was off work for a month as I was still feeling a bit weak.

Not long after starting back to work, it was end of the National Hunt season, and nearly all the horses were turned out into the paddocks. I went to stay and work at Wardington Lodge with Count and Countess Raben. Wardington is near Banbury in Oxfordshire and I stayed a couple of months before I returned to Major Dennistoun.

Whilst I was at Wardington I met Johnny Buckingham, the jockey who rode for Mrs Edward Courage, and later on in his career rode the winner of the Grand National on Foinavon. John and I became good friends.

Terrible Thing I Witness

One Sunday in the summer time Major Ginger Dennistoun asked me if I would go with him to Oaksey House because a farm labourer working there had become sick with a tummy bug and they needed to get the hay into the barn before the rains came.

So on this hot Sunday I went with the Major to Hill Farm to help. When we arrived, a tractor and trailer was all ready to go down to the fields. We all climbed on to the trailer. John "Lord Oaksey" shouted to us to wait a minute as we had forgotten the most important thing and then he ran back out carrying a crate of beer.

It was thirsty work and the beer was most appreciated by everyone. After the hay had all been put in the barn we were invited to stay for lunch. Afterwards Major Dennistoun said he would show me around the stable and gardens. When the Major and I walked to the other side of a new hedge, there lying on the ground were two young ladies wearing bikinis with their tops undone and the straps hanging loose.

The Major put his fingers to his lips and whispered, "Quiet." He then pulled out of his pocket a cigarette lighter, lit it and slowly crept up to the two ladies who were asleep and put the lit lighter under one of the ladies' big toes. Within a second or two the lady screamed and her body seem to go a foot into the air. The bikini top fell on the ground exposing her lovely breasts. The poor girl was shocked and started crying. The Major tried to console her by putting his arms around her. By this time people came running out to see what was happening. Lord Oaksey was telling the Major off and when I tried to leave, John turned on me saying, "You must think this is very funny."

I said I had no idea what the Major was going to do. The incident ruined the nice day.

"Lord Oaksey"(John Lawrence) Photos For Sunday Telegraph

When Lord Oaksey started to write for the Sunday Telegraph, Major Dennistoun told me that he would like me to come on a Sunday afternoon and ride with Lord Oaksey to have his photo taken for the newspaper.

On the appointed Sunday, John Lawrence and I met in the saddle room in the stable yard at Aitwick Manor in Leycombe Regis, which faces down the drive towards the "Mill House" lake. We stood waiting watching the camera men arriving. The Major came into the saddle room carrying a large bag. He put the bag down and told us to get changed into the jockey silks. John and I looked at each other. John said to the Major, "What colour silks would you like me to wear?"

The Major shouted back at John, "You silly ass, Fellhound is the horse that you will be riding. So you better put on Mr. Ben Smith's colours. He is the owner, come on we don't want to be here all day." Of course it was a bit embarrassing taking off your normal clothes and standing with only your underpants on.

When the door of the saddle room opened in came a camera man accompanied by a young lady.

The Major burst out, "Who do you think you are coming in here like that? Have you no manners at all. You should always knock on the door first." She went straight back out the door.

The Major turned to John Lawrence and said, "Look at you two, no wonder the woman ran straight out again. What a poor couple of human specimens you are. How come? Get your silks on. I am going out to see if Don

Mills (the head lad) has tacked up the horses for you both."

John and I carried on getting the silks on. But when we came to the riding boots, John could not pull his up over his calf muscle. His boot top was stuck. The Major came back into the saddle room saying "come on you two, off we go." But John still had not got his boots on. The Major looked at him.

"Why can't you get your boots on John?"

"Because they're too tight for me!"

"Ho, give the boots to me," said the Major. John handed over the boots and the Major put his hand in his pocket and brought out a small penknife - the knife he used for cleaning his pipe - and made a small cut at the back of the boots then handed them back to John.

"Well you know Sir Gordon Richards has large calves too."

"Well," replied the Major, "you will never be as good a jockey as he was as long as you have a hole in your ass!" I laughed.

We went out of saddle room and mounted the horses. The Major told us what we had to do. I was to follow John on his horse Fellhound, and stay with my horse's head just by his horse's quarters but not to go in front of him.

The camera men were dotted around the big paddock at the back of the stable yard. There must have been about five or more placed ten yards or so apart. It was hard work to keep the horses together. They whipped round when they got close to the camera men who were sitting on the ground. We had to keep cantering round the paddock and it took a long time before they said, 'that's enough'.

When I did see the photo they used for the Sunday Telegraph, it only had John on Fellhound. I was painted out! Just as well because I'm not photogenic!

Postscript

I have written this book to let people know how helpful Lord John Oaksey was to me and so many others. He always had the time for you and greeted you with a genuine smile. I will miss him a lot.

The large amount of people that attended his memorial services in London and at Oaksey village church showed the respect that people had for him.

Alwin 'Bobby' Watts

St Paul's Church
Wilton Place SW1

A Service of Thanksgiving for the Life of

JOHN GEOFFREY TRISTRAM LAWRENCE
BARON TREVETHIN AND OAKSEY

1929 – 2012

Wednesday, 7th November 2012

MURDER BY DESIGN:

The Unsane Cinema of Dario Argento

EL PAJARO DE LAS PLUMAS DE CRISTAL

TONY **MUSANTE**
SUZY **KENDALL**
ENRICO **MARIA SALERNO**
DIRECTOR
DARIO ARGENTO
EASTMANCOLOR TECHNISCOPE
70m/m Y 35 mm.

JANO.

MURDER BY DESIGN:

The Unsane Cinema of Dario Argento

by Troy Howarth

with the Special Collaboration of Rob Ruston

Midnight Marquee Press, Inc.
Baltimore, Maryland, U.S.A.

978-1-64430-116-6 Limited Edition Hardback   Library of Congress Catalog Card Number 2020949928
978-1-64430-114-2 Color Paperback   Library of Congress Catalog Card Number 2020950123
978-1-64430-115-9 Black and White Paperback   Library of Congress Catalog Card Number 2020950122

Manufactured in the United States of America

First Printing: November, 2020